DEDICAT

"...Dr. Prasad, I am very interested in your translation of Gita. **Though I have many English translations, I think your translation is the best one.** So far, there are 5 versions in China, and I hope we could translate your "Gita" into Chinese too.
   ---*Dr. Zhicheng Wang, Prof. of Religion and Philosophy.*

Premier Modi of India receiving our

Over 12,533 *** Stars reviews Chinese Gita**

(Eleventh print in China, Oct 2015-Nov

2019)
The most popular Gita translation in Chinese
To read more about the picture above, Click:

www.gita-society.com/pdf/china.pdf

.

.

THE BHAGAVAD-GITA

For Children

With Introduction, A Lucid, Simple
English Renditions of over 181 Simpler
Gita Verses, Illustrated With 26 Stories
and 14 pictures. Suitable For Children
Grades 8th and Above. A meditation
Technique and Simple mantras.

Ramananda Prasad, Ph.D.

INTERNATIONAL GITA SOCIETY

AIMS AND OBJECTIVES
International Gita Society
(Formerly: American Gita Society)

Founded in 1984, the International Gita Society (IGS) is a registered, non-profit, tax-exempt, spiritual institution in the United States of America under Section 501(c) (3) of the IRS Code. Membership is free of charge and open to all. The Aims and Objectives of IGS include:

1. Publish and distribute, The Bhagavad-Gita in simple and easy to understand languages, to anyone interested in the Gita.

2. Spread the basic Non-sectarian Universal teachings of Shrimad Bhagavad-Gita and other Vedic scriptures in easy to understand languages by establishing branches of the Society in other countries.

3. Provide support and guidance in establishing Gita Study and Discussion (Satsang) Groups, including a free Gita correspondence course.

4. To provide inspiration, cooperation, and support to persons and non-profit organizations engaged in the study and propagation of Vedic knowledge.

5. To break the barriers between faiths, and establish unity of races, religions, castes, and creeds through teachings of the Vedas, Upanishads, Gita, Ramayana, as well as other major world scriptures.

CONTACT: Phone: 1 510 791 6953

Buy our Paperbacks: www.gita-society.com/books.html

Buy this book from:

www.amazon.com/dp/1494268205/ **for only $5.99**

THE BHAGAVAD-GITA

Excerpts from reviews:

"….There is hardly any good publication on Gita's teachings for children. Dr. Prasad has done a **remarkable work for the children**. This book is written in a lucid style using the tradition of story telling by grandparents. **It teaches Gita to children in a loving manner** and will be a good beginning of a long journey to adulthood. **I congratulate Dr. Prasad for his dedication.**"

--- *Ved P. Vatuk*

" .... I would like to include the translation of the Gita by Dr. Ramananda Prasad in my site. I am interested in representing India fairly, and **I fear that the translation of the Gita by Sir Edwin Arnold that is distributed all over the net will do more to turn students away rather than introduce them fairly to the text….**"

---*Prof. Anthony Beavers, University of Evansville, Indiana.*

"… Prasad's deft renderings are elegantly simple, easy to understand and unencumbered by long commentary. **An ambitious work that will be appreciated by all who study the Gita** ... "

---- *Hinduism Today, USA*

"… Explanations of the theory and philosophy of selfless service has been so beautifully expounded …."

--- *Prof. S. Tilak, Concordia University, Canada.*

Second Children Edition, 2016
Fifth (Paperback) Edition, 2012
First e-book edition, 2012
Fourth Edition, Second Printing, 2008
First (Pocket Paperback) Edition, 2008
First Children Edition, 2008
Fourth Revised and Enlarged Edition, 2004
First Hindi Edition, 2004
(Published by Motilal Banarsidass in India)
Free Pocket size editions, 2000-2012
Third Revised Edition, 1999
Third and other Printings, 1998
Second Printing, 1997
Second Revised and Enlarged Edition, 1996
 (Published by Motilal Banarsidass in India)
First Edition, 1988

ISBN 13: **978 149 426 8206**
ISBN 10: 149 426 8205

Copyright © 2020 by the
International Gita Society
511 Lowell Place, Fremont, CA 94536
Phone (510) 791 6953
sanjay@gita-society.com
Visit: www.gita-society.com

Writer: Ramananda Prasad, Ph.D.
Editors: Doret Kollerer for English
            Yashodara Singh, Ph.D. for Hindi
Graphics and Consulting: Madhavacharya (Michael Beloved)

Editorial Board:

Sadhana Prasad, Kalavati Patel, Sunita Singh, Reeta Raina, Sanjay Prasad, Usha Gupta, Jay Raina, Raj Raina.

A short note on pronunciation:

"ā" is hard "a" sound as in Rāma. letter "a" in Sanskrit words is soft "a" as in Albert. It is different from "ā" sound and is either not pronounced or pronounced very very softly.

International Gita Society

CONTENTS

THE BHAGAVAD-GITA
(For Children and Beginners)

NOTE: *For better understanding, this scripture of the Bhagavad-Gita should be learned by the beginners with adult help.*

INTRODUCTION

Jay: Grandma, I have a hard time understanding the teachings of the Bhagavad-Gita. Would you help me?

Grandma: Of course, Jay, I will be glad to. You should know that this holy book teaches us how to live happily in the world. It is an ancient holy book of Hindu Dharma (also known as Sanātana Dharma or Hinduism), but it can be understood and followed by people of any faith. The Gita has eighteen (18) chapters and a total of only 700 verses. Anyone can be helped by daily practice of only a few of its teachings.

The word 'Bhagavad' means God or The Supreme Lord, Bhagavān in Sanskrit. 'Gita' means song. Thus The Bhagavad-Gita means the Song of God or the Sacred Song, because it was sung by Bhagavān Shri Krishna himself.

Here is an introduction to the Gita:

In ancient times there was a king who had two sons, Dhritarāshtra and Pāndu. The former was born blind; therefore, Pāndu inherited the kingdom. Pāndu had five sons. They were called the Pāndavas. Dhritarāshtra had one hundred sons. They were called the Kauravas. Duryodhana was the eldest of the Kauravas.

After the death of king Pāndu, his eldest son, Yudhisthira, became the lawful King. Duryodhana was very jealous. He also wanted the kingdom. The kingdom was divided into two halves between the Pāndavas and the Kauravas. Duryodhana was not satisfied with his share. He wanted the entire kingdom for himself. He tried several evil plots to kill the Pāndavas and take away their kingdom. Somehow he took over the entire kingdom of the Pāndavas and refused to give it back without a war. All peace talks by Lord Krishna and others failed, so the big war of Mahābhārata could not be avoided.

The Pāndavas didn't want to fight, but they had only two choices: fight for their right because it was their duty or run away from war and accept defeat for the sake of peace and nonviolence. Arjuna, one of the five Pāndava brothers, faced this choice in the battlefield.

He had to choose between fighting the war and killing his most revered guru, who was on the other side; his very dear friends, close relatives, and many innocent warriors; or running away from the battlefield to be peaceful and nonviolent. The entire eighteen chapters of the Gita are the talk between confused Arjuna and his best friend, mentor and cousin, Lord Krishna — an incarnation of God — on the battlefield of Kurukshetra near New Delhi, India, about 5,100 years ago. This conversation was reported to the blind king, Dhritarāshtra, by his charioteer, Sanjay. It is recorded in the great epic, Mahābhārata.

All lives, human or nonhuman, are sacred, and nonviolence or Ahimsā is one of the most basic principles of Hinduism. So when Lord Krishna advises Arjuna to get up and fight, this may confuse you about the principle of Ahimsā if you don't keep in mind the background of the war of Mahābhārata.

This spiritual talk between the Supreme Lord, Krishna, and His devotee-friend, Arjuna, occurs not in a temple, a lonely forest, or on a mountain top, but on a battlefield on the eve of a war.

Jay: This is an interesting story, Grandma. Can you tell me more?

Grandma: If you come to where I sit every evening, Jay, I will tell you the whole story, one chapter each day. Just make sure your homework is done and you have time to listen. If you agree, let's start tomorrow.

Jay: Thank you, Grandma. I'll be there to hear more.

CHAPTER 1
ARJUNA'S CONFUSION

Jay: I would like to know first how Lord Krishna and Arjuna happened to talk on the battlefield, Grandma.

Grandma: It came about in this way, Jay. The war of Mahābhārata was about to begin after peace talks by Lord Krishna and others failed to avoid the war. When the soldiers were gathered on the battlefield, Arjuna asked Lord Krishna to drive his chariot between the two armies so that he could see those who were ready to fight. Seeing all his relatives, friends, and soldiers on the battlefield and fearing their destruction, he became compassionate.

Jay: What does compassionate mean, Grandma?

Grandma: Compassion does not mean pity, Jay. That would be looking down on others as poor, pitiful creatures. Arjuna was feeling their pain and their unlucky situation as his own. Arjuna was a great warrior, who had fought many wars and was well prepared for the war, but suddenly his compassion made him not want to fight. He spoke of the evils of war and sat down on the seat of his chariot, his mind full of sorrow. He saw no use in fighting. He did not know what to do.

Jay: I don't blame him. I wouldn't want to fight either. Why do people fight, Grandma? Why are there wars?

Grandma: Jay, there are not only wars between nations, but quarrels between two people, quarrels between brothers and sisters, between husband and wife, between friends and neighbors. The main reason is that people are not able to let go of their selfish motives and desires. Most wars are fought for possession and power. But all problems could be solved peacefully if people could see both sides of the problem and work out an agreement. War should be the last resort. Our holy books say: One should not commit violence towards anyone. Unjustified killing is punishable in all circumstances. Lord Krishna urged Arjuna to fight for his rights, but not to kill needlessly. It was his duty as a warrior to fight a declared war and establish peace and law and order on earth.

We humans also have wars going inside all of us. Our negative and positive forces are always fighting. The negative forces within us are represented by the Kauravas and the positive forces by the Pāndavas. The Gita does not have stories in it to illustrate the teachings, so I will add some stories from other sources to help you.

Here is a story about negative and positive thoughts fighting each other that Lord Krishna Himself told to Arjuna in Mahābhārata.

1. Mr. Truthful

There once lived a great hermit, who was famous for telling the truth. He had taken a vow not to lie and was popularly known as "Mr. Truthful." No matter what he said, everyone believed him because he had earned a great reputation in the community where he lived and did his spiritual practices.

One evening, a robber was chasing a merchant to rob and kill him. The merchant was running for his life. To escape from the robber, the merchant ran towards the forest where the hermit lived outside the village.

The merchant felt very safe because there was no way the robber could find out where he was hiding in the jungle. But the hermit had seen the direction in which the merchant went.

The robber came to the hermit's cottage and paid his respects. The robber knew that the hermit would tell only the truth and could be trusted, so he asked him whether he had seen somebody running away. The hermit knew that the robber must be looking for somebody to rob and kill, so he faced a big problem. If he told the truth, the merchant would certainly be killed. If he lied, he would incur the sin of lying and lose his reputation. Any immoral act that may harm others is called sin. Ahimsā (nonviolence) and truthfulness are two most important teachings of all religions that we must follow. If we have to choose between these two, which one should we choose? This is a very difficult choice.

Because of his habit of telling the truth, the hermit said: "Yes, I saw someone going that way." So the robber was able to find the merchant and kill him. The hermit could have saved a life by hiding the truth, but he did not think very carefully and made a wrong decision.

Lord Krishna's purpose in telling Arjuna this story was to teach Arjuna that sometimes we have to choose between a rock and a hard place. Lord Krishna told Arjuna that the hermit shared with the robber the sin of killing a life. The robber could not have found the merchant if the hermit had not told the truth. So when two noble principles conflict with each other, we have to know which one is the higher principle. Ahimsa has the highest priority, so the hermit should have lied in this situation to save a life. One may not tell a truth that harms a person in any way. It isn't easy to apply Dharma (or righteousness) to real life situations because what is Dharma and what is Adharma (or unrighteousness) can sometimes be very difficult to decide. In such a situation, expert advice should be sought.

Lord Krishna gave another example of a robber coming to a village to rob and kill the villagers. In this situation, killing the robber would be an act of nonviolence because killing one person may save many lives. Lord Krishna Himself, on several occasions, had to make such decisions to win the war of Mahābhārata and put an end to all the evil-doers.

Remember, Jay, do not tell a lie, and do not kill any living being or hurt anybody, but saving a life comes first.

Chapter 1 summary: Arjuna asked his charioteer friend, Lord Krishna, to drive his chariot between the two armies so that he could see the Pāndava's army. Arjuna felt great compassion to see his friends and relatives on the opposite side, whom he must kill to win the war. He became confused, spoke of the evils of war, and refused to fight.

CHAPTER 2
KNOWLEDGE OF GOD

Jay: If Arjuna felt so kind-hearted for everyone he was supposed to kill in the war, how could he go out and fight, Grandma?

Grandma: That is exactly what Arjuna asked Lord Krishna. He said: "How shall I strike my grandfather, my guru, and all other relatives with arrows in battle? They are worthy of my respect" (Gita **2.04**).
(in Gita 2.04: 2 is Chapter number, 04 is Verse number)
    Arjuna had a good point. In Vedic culture, gurus, the elderly, honorable persons, and all other superiors are to be respected. But the scriptures also say that anyone who acts wrongly or unlawfully against you or others, or anyone who supports such deeds, should no longer be respected, but punished.
    Arjuna was confused about his duty and asked guidance from Lord Krishna. Lord Krishna then instructed him on the true knowledge of Atmā and the physical body.

Jay: What is Atmā, Grandma?

Grandma: Atmā is also called the Spirit, or the soul. Atmā is never born, never dies, and is everlasting. Our body takes birth and dies, but not Atmā. Atmā supports the body. Without Atmā, the body becomes dead. Atmā supplies the power to our body, mind, and senses, just as air burns and supports fire. Weapons cannot cut Atmā, fire cannot burn it, wind cannot dry it, and water cannot make it wet. Therefore, we should not grieve over death of the body because the Atmā inside the body never dies (Gita 2.23-24).

Jay: What is the difference between Atmā (Spirit), soul, and body Grandma?

Grandma: One and the same Atmā dwells inside all bodies. Our body changes with time. Our old-age body is different from our childhood body. But Atmā does not change. Atmā takes a childhood body, a youth body, and an old-age body during this life, then takes another body after death (Gita 2.13). The Sanskrit word Atmā is translated as Spirit in English. Spirit is universal and all pervading. The English word spirit or soul also means the Spirit residing in individual bodies. In Sanskrit language, we call this individual soul Jivātmā or Jiva (also spelled as Jeeva). If Spirit is compared to a forest, the individual soul (spirit or Jiva) can be compared to the tree in the forest.

The body is called a garment of Atmā. Just as we get rid of an old, worn-out garment and put on a new one, similarly, Atmā gets rid of the old body and takes a new one after death. So death is like changing the garment of Atmā (Gita 2.22). All beings are visible between birth and death; they can't be seen before birth or after death and remain in their invisible form (Gita 2.28). Therefore, we should not grieve over death of the body. We are not the body. We are Atmā with a body. Death just means our soul passes from one body to another new body.

Jay: Then why did Arjuna grieve over deaths of loved ones on the battlefield? Why didn't he want

to fight?

Grandma: Arjuna was a very tough warrior, Jay, but he wanted to run away from the horrors of war and lead an easy life of a Samnyāsi, a wandering hermit. Lord Krishna taught us to face the battle of life by giving Arjuna the beautiful science of KarmaYoga, the art of peaceful and prosperous living. Chapter 3 of the Gita tells us more about this. Arjuna was worried about the results of the war, but Lord Krishna asks us to do our duty without worrying too much about the results, such as gain and loss, victory and defeat, success and failure. If you are constantly worried about the results of your studies, you will not be able to put your heart and soul into them for fear of failure.

Jay: But Grandma, how could Arjuna fight his best if he wasn't fighting to win and gain something?

Grandma: Arjuna must fight to win, but he should not weaken his will by worrying about the result while he is fighting. He should put all his attention and energy into every minute of the fight. That energy is what will bring the greatest result.

   Lord Krishna tells us that we have full control over our action, but no control over the results of our action (Gita 2.47). Harry Bhalla says: A farmer has control over how he works his land, yet no control over the harvest. But he cannot expect a harvest if he does not work his land with best effort and with tools he has.

   We should do our best at the present moment and let the future take care of itself.

Jay: Could you tell me more about the secret of success as told by Krishna to Arjuna?

Grandma: We should be so completely absorbed in work or study as to become unaware of everything else, even of its results. To achieve the best results from what we do, we should be focused on the action with undivided attention.

Action should be done sincerely without worrying about its results. The results of the action will be greater if we put all attention and energy into the action itself and do not allow our energy to be diverted by thinking of results. The result will depend on energy put into action. We are asked not to worry about results during the course of action. This does not mean that we should not care about results. But we should not expect only positive results all the time.

The secret of living a meaningful life is to be very active, and do our best without thinking of our own selfish motives or even the results. A Self-realized person works for the good of all.

Jay: What is a Self-realized person like, Grandma?

Grandma: A Self-realized person is a perfect person, Jay. Lord Krishna tells us the mind of a perfect person is not shaken by difficulties, does not run after pleasures, is free from fear, desire, greed, and attachment, and has control over mind and senses (Gita 2.56). A Self-realized person does not get angry, is peaceful and happy.

Jay: How can we keep from getting angry, Grandma?

Grandma: We get angry if our desire is not fulfilled (Gita 2.62). So the best way to control anger is to control or limit our desires. We should not want too many things. Desires begin in the mind, so we should control our mind. If we don't control our mind, we drift like a ship without its rudder. The desire for pleasure takes one to the dark alley of sin, gets us in trouble, and prevents our progress (Gita 2.67). As a student, you should set a higher goal for yourself than pleasure. Put forth your best effort and concentrate on your studies.

Arjuna was a very good example of such concentration. Here is a story about him.

2. The Graduation Test

Guru Drona was the military teacher for both the Kauravas and the Pāndavas. At the end of their military training came final examination time. Drona put a wooden eagle on the branch of a nearby tree. Nobody knew it was just a doll. It looked like a real eagle. To pass the graduation test, every one of the students was supposed to cut off the eagle's head with one arrow.

Guru Drona first asked Yudhisthira, the eldest of the Pāndavas: "Get ready, look at the eagle, and tell me what you are seeing."

Yudhisthira replied: "I see the sky, the clouds, the tree trunk, the branches, the leaves and the eagle sitting there"

Guru Drona was not very pleased with this answer. He asked the same of all the students, one by one. Every one of them gave a similar answer. Then came Arjuna's turn for the test.

Drona asked Arjuna: "Get ready, look at the eagle, and tell me what you are seeing."

Arjuna replied: "I only see the eagle and nothing else"

Drona then asked a second question: "If you are seeing the eagle, then tell me how strong is its body and what is the color of it's wings?"

Arjuna replied: "I am only seeing its head and not the entire body."

Guru Drona was much pleased with Arjuna's answer and asked him to go ahead with the test. Arjuna easily cut off the head of the eagle with one arrow because he was concentrating on his aim with a single mind. He passed the test with flying colors.

Arjuna was not only the greatest warrior of his time, but also a compassionate KarmaYogi. Lord Krishna chose Arjuna as a medium to impart the knowledge of the holy Gita.

We all should follow the example of Arjuna. Read the Gita and be like Arjuna. "Arjuna Bano, Arjuna Bano," my dear grandson! Whatever work you do, do it with single-minded attention and put your whole heart and mind into it. This is the main theme of KarmaYoga of the Gita and the secret of success in anything you do.

A word for the youth from Swami Vivekananda:

"Whatever you are doing, put your whole mind on it. If you are shooting, your mind should be only on the target. Then you will never miss. If you are learning your lessons, think only of the lesson. In India boys and girls are taught to do this".

Chapter 2 summary: Lord Krishna taught us, through Arjuna, the difference between Atmā and body. We are Atmā with a body. Atmā is unborn and indestructible. One and the same Atmā dwells inside all bodies, human or nonhuman. Thus we are all connected with each other. We should do our duty to the best of our ability without worrying about success or failure. We must learn from our failures and go forward without letting our failures defeat us. To become a perfect person, we need to control or limit our desires.

CHAPTER 3
PATH OF SOCIAL SERVICE

Jay: Why do we have to control our desires, Grandma?

Grandma: When you choose wrong behavior for sense enjoyment, you also choose its results. That is why work has to be done for the welfare of all and not just to satisfy your desires or for personal gain. One who practices KarmaYoga is called a KarmaYogi. A KarmaYogi finds the right way to serve and turns her or his work into worship. In KarmaYoga, no work is more important or less important than other work.

Jay: Uncle Hari left his family and home and went to an Ashram last year to find God. Do we have to leave home to seek God?

Grandma: No, we do not. In the Gita, Lord Krishna has given us different paths to God-realization. The path you choose depends on your individual nature. In general, there are two types of people in the world: the inward (or studious, introvert) type and the outward or active type. For the introvert like Uncle Hari, the path of spiritual knowledge is best. Followers of this path go to a spiritual master or a guru where they study Vedic scriptures under proper guidance. In this path, we learn who we are and how we can lead a happy and peaceful life.

Jay: Do we have to read all the scriptures to understand and find God?

Grandma: There are many scriptures in our religion, such as the 4 Vedas, 108 Upanishads, 18 Purānas, Rāmāyanas, Mahābhārata, various Sutras and many others. Reading all of them would be a difficult task. But Lord Krishna has given us everything we need to know about God in the Gita. The Gita has the essence of all the Vedas and Upanishads for the modern time.

Jay: Uncle Puri is a farmer and has no interest in studying the Gita. He says the Gita is difficult and not for common people like him. So how can Uncle Puri realize God?

Grandma: Uncle Puri should follow the second path, the path of KarmaYoga that is described in this chapter of the Gita. This is the path of duty or selfless service. This path is better for most people who work hard to support a family and have no time or interest to read scriptures. Followers of this path do not have to
leave work and go to an Ashram. They give up selfish motives and do all work for the greater good of society, instead of just for themselves.

Jay: But people will work harder if they have selfish motives, won't they, Grandma?

Grandma: It is true that people may earn more if they work for selfish gain, but they will not find permanent peace and happiness. Only those who do their duty selflessly for the good of all people will find real peace and satisfaction.

Jay: If people don't work for personal gain, will they still do their best and not become lazy?

Grandma: A true KarmaYogi works hard even without personal gain. Only the ignorant work just for personal gain. The world runs smoothly because people do their duty. Parents work hard to support their family, and the children do their part. Nobody can remain inactive or idle all the time. Most people engage in some activity and do what they can. Brahmā, the creator, gave his first teaching to humanity when he said: Let all of you progress and prosper by helping each other and by doing your duty properly (Gita 3.10-11).

Jay: What happens if people work hard just for their own benefit?

Grandma: They commit sin, Jay. It is wrong to perform any action selfishly without considering its effect on others. Lord Krishna calls such a person a thief, useless, and sinful (Gita 3.12-13). We should never live and work just for ourselves. We should help and serve each other.

Jay: What does a person gain who follows the teaching of Lord Brahmā and works for the good of society?

Grandma: Such a person attains peace and success in this life, reaches God, and does not take birth again on this earth.

Here is a true modern story of how selfless service, discussed in Chapter 3, works wonders in life.

3. Sir Alexander Fleming

A poor Scottish farmer one day, while trying to make a living for his family, heard a cry for help coming from a nearby swamp. He dropped his tools and ran to the bog.

There, sunk to his waist in the swamp, was a terrified boy, screaming and struggling to free himself. Farmer Fleming saved the lad from what could have been a slow and terrifying death.

The next day, a fancy carriage pulled up to the Scotsman's simple home. A well dressed nobleman stepped out and introduced himself as the father of the boy that Farmer Fleming had saved.

"I want to thank and repay you," said the nobleman. "You saved my son's life."

"I can't accept payment for what I did," the Scottish farmer replied, rejecting the offer.

At that moment, the farmer's own son came to the door of the family hovel.

"Is that your son?" the nobleman asked.

"Yes," the farmer replied proudly.

"I'll make you a deal. Let me provide him with the level of education my own son will enjoy. If the lad is anything like his father, he'll no doubt grow to be a man we both will be proud of."

And that he did. Farmer Fleming's son attended the very best schools and in time graduated from St. Mary's Hospital Medical School in London and went on to become known throughout the world as the noted Sir Alexander Fleming, the discoverer of Penicillin.

Years afterward, the same nobleman's son who was saved from the swamp was stricken with pneumonia. What saved his life this time? Penicillin.

The name of the nobleman? Lord Randolph Churchill.

His son's name? The famous Sir Winston Churchill.

Someone once said: What goes around comes around. This is the universal law of Karma, the law of cause and effect. Help fulfill someone's dream, and your dream shall be fulfilled too by the Lord!

Jay: Please give me more examples of true KarmaYogis, Grandma.

Grandma: You have read the story of Rāmāyana. Lord Rāma's father-in-law was Janaka, the King of Janakpur in the state of Bihar, India. He attained God by serving his people as his own children, selflessly and without attachment to the results of his action. He did his duty as worship of God. Work done without any selfish motive, as a matter of duty, becomes worship of God because it helps God run the world.

Mahātmā Gandhi was a true KarmaYogi, who worked selflessly all his life without any personal motive, just for the good of society. He set an example for other world leaders to follow. There are many other examples of selfless persons.

Jay: Is that how our leaders should work?

Grandma: Yes, a true KarmaYogi shows by personal example how to lead a selfless life and attain God by following the path of KarmaYoga (Gita 3.21).

Jay: If I want to become a KarmaYogi, what do I have to do?

Grandma: KarmaYoga requires doing our duty in life the best we can, unselfishly, without attachment to the results of our work. A KarmaYogi remains calm in both success and failure and has no likes or dislikes for any person, place, object, or work. Work done as selfless service for the welfare of humanity produces no good or bad Kārmic bondage and leads one to God.

Jay: It would be hard to work without wanting something personally from it. How do we do this?

Grandma: Spiritually ignorant persons work just for themselves. The wise work for the welfare of all. The ignorant work to enjoy the result of their labor and become attached to it because they think they are the doer. They do not realize that all work is done by the power supplied to us by God. With the power to do our duty and the intellect to choose between right and wrong action, we become responsible for our actions. People act wrongly because they don't use their intellect and don't think of the results of their action on others.

The wise offer all their work to God with no selfish desire of their own. The ignorant work only to fulfill their personal desires (Gita 3.25).

Jay: Can a common person like me do what great people like King Janaka and Mahātmā Gandhi have done?

Grandma: With a little effort, anybody can follow the path of KarmaYoga. Think of whatever work you are doing as your gift to society. If you are a student, your duty is to attend school, do your homework, respect your parents, teachers, other elders, and help your brothers, sisters, friends, and classmates. In student life, prepare yourself to be a good, productive citizen by getting a good education.

Jay: What kind of work should I do when I graduate, Grandma?

Grandma: Choose the work that you like and can do well. The work should be suited to your nature (Gita 3.35, 18.47). If you choose work for which you don't have a natural skill or attraction, your chances of success are limited. You know what you can do best. Trying to be someone you're not is the greatest cause of failure and unhappiness.

Jay: But shouldn't I try to find good work, like engineering, teaching, or government service?

Grandma: There is no such thing as good or bad work. All types of workers are needed to keep society running. Some work pays more than others, but higher paying jobs are usually more difficult and stressful if you are not qualified for them. If you are qualified for a lower paying job, lead a simple life and avoid unnecessary items. A simple life means not desiring too many material things. Limit yourself to the basic needs of life. Keep your desires under control. Lord Buddha said: Selfish desire is the cause of all evils and misery.

Jay: Is selfish desire the reason why people do bad things?
Grandma: Yes Jay, our selfish desire for enjoyment is the cause of all evils. If we don't control our desires, our desires will control us, and we will become the victims of our own desires. Control your wants because whatever you want, wants you also!

Jay: Then are all desires bad?

Grandma: No, all desires are not bad. The desire to serve others is a noble desire. The desire to enjoy pleasures is bad because it leads to sinful and illegal activities. Always remember that desire never ends after you get what you want. It just leads to new desires and creates greed. And if you don't get what you want, you feel angry. People do bad things when they are angry.

Jay: How can we control our desire for pleasures?

Grandma: One way is by the knowledge given in the Gita and by the power of thinking. Before you act to fulfill your desire, always think first of the results of that action. Desires start in the mind and stay there. You can control your mind by intellect and reasoning.

When you are young, your mind becomes dirty just as the clear water of a pond becomes muddy during the rainy season. If your intellect doesn't control your mind, your mind will run after sense pleasures. This will keep you from achieving the higher goals of life. So set a high goal in life to keep your mind from getting dirty by sensual pleasures like smoking, alcohol, drugs, and other bad habits. Bad habits are very hard to get rid of, so avoid them to start with. Always keep good company, read good books, avoid bad people, and think of the long-term result of your actions.

Jay: Since we know right from wrong, Grandma, why can't we just avoid doing wrong?

Grandma: If we don't control our mind, it will try to weaken our will and take us for a ride to the wrong road of sensual pleasures. We have to watch our mind and keep it on track.

Chapter 3 Summary: Lord Krishna mentioned two major paths to peace and happiness in life. The path chosen depends on the individual. It is easy for most people to follow the path of KarmaYoga, the path of selfless service. To help each other is the first teaching of the creator. This keeps society going and progressing. We should all do our duty to the best of our ability. Choose the career best suited to your nature. No job is small. It's not what you

do, but how you do it that is important. Finally, Lord Krishna tells us we must control our desire for pleasures. Uncontrolled desires for pleasure lead us to failure and suffering in life. We must think about the results of an action before taking it up. Avoid bad company at all costs.

CHAPTER 4
RENUNCIATION WITH KNOWLEDGE

Jay: The Gita reports what was spoken on the battlefield, but who wrote it, Grandma?

Grandma: The teachings of the Gita are very old. They were first given to the Sun-god in the beginning of creation by Lord Krishna. Over time, this knowledge got lost. The Gita in its present form is the teaching by the Supreme Lord, Krishna, to Arjuna about 5,100 years ago.

Jay: So is Lord Krishna the author of the Gita?

Grandma: Yes, Lord Krishna is the author of the Gita. It was put together by sage Vayāsa who also edited the four Vedas. Sage Vayāsa had the power of recalling events of the past and future, but he could not do the work of both composing as well as writing it down. He needed a helper to write the Mahābhārata. Lord Ganesha, the lord of wisdom, offered to do the work of writing.

The Gita was first translated from the original

Sanskrit poetry to Sanskrit prose and fully explained in Sanskrit by great guru Adi Shankarāchārya in the year 800 A.D.

Jay: Why is Lord Krishna so important?

Grandma: Lord Krishna is considered the eighth incarnation of the Supreme God.

Ten Incarnations of Lord Vishnu

The Supreme God comes to earth in different forms from time to time whenever the forces of evil try to disturb and destroy the world peace. Lord comes to set everything right (Gita 4.07-08). He also sends prophets and teachers to help mankind. His birth and activities are divine and each incarnation (Avatāras) has a purpose. The Shrimad Bhāgavatam (or the Bhāgavad-Purāna) gives details of all ten major Avatāras (incarnations) of God. All saints and sages of other religions are also considered minor incarnations of God. At the end of the present time period, known as KaliYuga, the Kalki incarnation will happen in about 427,000 years from now.

Jay: Will Lord Krishna give us whatever we want in prayer or worship?

Grandma: Yes, Lord Krishna will give what you want (Gita 4.11), such as success in your study, if you worship Him with faith. People may worship and pray to God by using any name and form of God. The form of God is called deity. One can also worship God without the help of a deity.

Jay: Will we still have to study if we want to do well in examinations?

Grandma: Yes, you must do the work. Do your best and then pray. The good Lord will not work for you. You will have to do your own work. Your work should be free from selfish desires, and you should not hurt anybody. Then you will not earn any Karma.

Jay: What is Karma, Grandma?

Grandma: The Sanskrit word Karma means action. It also means the results of an action. The word Karma is most commonly mispronounced as Karmā. Every action produces a result called Karma, which can be good or bad. If we do our work only to enjoy the results ourselves, we become responsible for the results. If our action harms anyone, we get bad Karma, called sin, and we will have to suffer in hell for it. If we do good to others, we earn good Karma and get rewarded by a trip to heaven.

Our own Karma is responsible for our rebirth to enjoy or suffer the results of our deeds. Karma is like depositing money in the form of good and bad action in the bank. We do not take birth when all our Karma, good or bad, is used up. This freedom from the cycles of birth and death is called liberation, Nirvāna, Moksha or Mukti. In Mukti one becomes one with God.

Jay: How can we avoid Karma when we live and work in society?

Grandma: The best way not to earn any Karma is not to do anything just for yourself, but do it for the good of society. Always keep in mind that Mother Nature does everything; we are not the real doer of any action. If we strongly believe this and work as a servant of God, we will not earn any new Karma, and all our past Karma will be wiped out by Spiritual knowledge. When all Karma is used up, we become liberated. This method of uniting with God is called the path of selfless action (KarmaYoga).

Jay How do we get rid of the Karma from our past lives?

Grandma: A very good question! True knowledge of the Self (or God) acts like fire that burns away all Karma from our past lives (Gita 4.37). Selfless service (KarmaYoga) prepares one to receive Self-knowledge. A KarmaYogi automatically gets Self-knowledge in due course of time (Gita 4.38). One who has true knowledge of the Self or God is called a Self-realized or a God-realized person.

Jay: Are there other ways to get liberation, Grandma?

Grandma: Yes, Jay, there are different methods or ways to reach God. These methods are called spiritual practices or Sādhanā. Any action that is beneficial to society is also called Yajna, Sevā or sacrifice. Different types of Yajna are: (1) giving money as charity for a good cause, (2) doing meditation, worship and yogic exercises, (3) reading the scriptures to gain knowledge of God, and (4) having control over the mind and other five senses (Gita 4.28).

Lord is pleased by those who sincerely perform any one of these Yajna and gives them the gift of Self-knowledge to reach God. Such a person becomes happy and peaceful (Gita 4.39).

Jay: How about those who just worship a deity everyday? Can they also reach God?
Grandma: Yes, those who worship the deity with full faith also get whatever they want (Gita 4.11-12). Most Hindus worship God in the form of a chosen deity to fulfill their desires. This path is known as path of worship and prayer. There is a story in the Mahābhārata of a devoted KarmaYogi and an ideal student who worshipped his guru and got what he wanted.

4. Ekalavya, the Ideal Student

Guru Dronāchārya (or Drona) was the military teacher (guru) appointed by grandfather Bhishma for all the Kaurava and Pāndava brothers. Many other princes also took military training under him. Drona was very much pleased by Arjuna's personal service and devotion to him, and he promised him: "I will train you to be the best archer in the world."

One day a very gentle boy named Ekalavya from a nearby village came to Drona and wanted to learn archery from him. He had heard from his mother about master archer Dronāchārya, who was the son of the sage Bhāradvāja and a disciple of sage Parashurāma.

Ekalavya was a jungle boy, belonging to the hunters' community. Then, and even today, such communities were considered socially inferior. Drona was worried how he could teach a jungle boy along with the royal children. So he decided not to keep the boy with him there, and told him: "Son, it will be very difficult for me to teach you. But you are a born archer. Go back to the forest and practice well with deep interest. You too are my disciple. May you master archery as you wish!"

Drona's words were a great blessing to Ekalavya. He understood his helplessness and felt confident that the Master's good wishes were with him. He made a clay idol of Dronāchārya, installed it in a nice place, and began to worship it respectfully by offering flowers, fruits, etc. He worshipped this idol of his guru everyday, practiced the lessons in archery in the Master's absence, and mastered the art.

Ekalavya would get up early in the morning, bathe himself and offer worship to the master's idol. He cherished the words, actions, and training methods of Drona that he had seen at guru Drona's Ashram. He faithfully followed the instructions and continued his practice.

While Arjuna had personally mastered archery from Drona, learning from him firsthand, Ekalavya achieved equally impressive skill while worshiping the Master from far away. If he could not do a particular technique, he would rush to Drona's image, present his problem and meditate until a solution appeared in his mind. He would then proceed further.

The story of Ekalavya demonstrates that one can

achieve anything in life if one has faith and works sincerely to reach the goal. The story continues:

The Kaurava and Pāndava princes once went to the forest on a hunting trip. Their leading dog was running forward. Ekalavya, a dark-skinned young man dressed in a tiger skin and wearing strings of conch-beads, was engaged in his practice. The dog, on approaching him, began to bark. Probably wishing to show off his skill, Ekalavya sent down a series of seven arrows in the direction of the barking dog, and his arrows filled its mouth. The dog ran back to the princes, who were surprised at this skill in archery and wondered who the archer was.

Arjuna, seeing this, was not only surprised but also worried. He wanted to be known as the world's best archer.

The princes went in search of the archer who had hit their dog with so many arrows in such a short time, and found Ekalavya.

Arjuna said: "Your skill in archery is great. Who is your guru?"

"My guru is Dronāchārya," replied Ekalavya humbly.

Arjuna was shocked at the mention of Drona's name. Was this true? Could his dear teacher teach so much to this boy? If so, what about the Master's promise to him? When did Drona teach the boy? Arjuna had never seen Ekalavya before in his class.

When Drona heard this story, he remembered Ekalavya and went to see him.

Drona said: "Your learning has been very good, son. I am deeply satisfied. With devotion and practice, you have done very well. May your achievement become an example for all to follow."

Ekalavya was very happy and said: "Thank you, oh Gurudeva! I too am a disciple of yours. Otherwise, I do not know whether I could have done this much."

Drona said: "If you accept me as your Master, you must pay my fee after your training. Think it over."

Ekalavya smilingly replied: "What is there to think over, Sir? I am your disciple, and you are my guru. Please say what you wish, Sir. I will fulfill it even if I have to sacrifice my life in the effort."

"Ekalavya, I have to demand a supreme sacrifice from you to fulfill my word to Bhishma and Arjuna that nobody would ever equal Arjuna in archery. Pardon me, son! Can you give me the thumb of your right hand as my fee?"

Ekalavya stared at Dronāchārya for a while. He could understand the Master's problem. He then stood up, walked to the Drona's idol with determination, placed his right thumb upon a stone, and cut it off in an instant, using his left hand and an arrow.

Drona, while feeling sorry for the injury he had caused Ekalavya, was at the same time deeply touched by such great devotion. He hugged him saying: "Son, your love for guru is unmatched. I feel a sense of fulfillment in having had a disciple like you. May God bless you!"

Ekalavya got victory in defeat! With the right thumb gone, he could no longer use the bow effectively. But he continued his practice using his left arm. By virtue of his supreme sacrifice, he received the grace of God and achieved distinction as a left-handed archer. He proved that nothing could stop a totally sincere effort. By his actions and behavior, Ekalavya, showed that your inferior or superior status is not determined by the community you belong to but by your vision and qualities of mind and heart.

Drona was a great guru, Jay. But there are many false gurus in the world who will try to cheat you.

Jay: Do we need a guru to reach God?

Grandma: We definitely need a teacher to learn any subject, spiritual or material such as music, science, Algebra. But to find a real guru or a spiritual guide is not so easy. There are four types of gurus: the knower of a subject or a teacher (guru), a false guru, a SadGuru and a ParamGuru. There are many false gurus who just pose as a guru. SadGuru is a God-realized master and is very hard to find. Lord Krishna is called the JagadGuru or ParamaGuru, the world-teacher.

When you graduate from a college and enter family life, you will need to find a real Guru or a true spiritual guide. Be very careful in choosing a Guru.

Chapter 4 summary: Lord comes to earth from time to time in a life-form to set things right on the earth. The Lord fulfills the desires of those who worship Him. There are four types of spiritual practices or Yajna. Both selfless service and Self-knowledge free the soul from the bondage of Karma. The Lord gives Self-knowledge to those who do selfless service. Self-knowledge burns all our past Karma and frees us from the wheel or cycles of birth and death.

CHAPTER 5
THE PATH OF RENUNCIATION

Jay: Previously, you mentioned two paths. Which path is better for most people, Grandma, the path of spiritual knowledge or the path of selfless service?

Grandma: A person who has the true knowledge of God believes that all work is done by the energy of Mother Nature and he or she is not the real doer of an action. Such a person is called a Samnyāsi or renunciant and has Self-knowledge. A KarmaYogi works without a selfish motive for the fruits of work. KarmaYoga prepares one to receive Self-knowledge (Gita 4.38, 5.06). Self-knowledge leads to renunciation. Thus selfless service or KarmaYoga forms the basis of renunciation (Samnyāsa). Both paths finally lead to God. Lord Krishna considers KarmaYoga the better of the two paths because it is faster and easier for most people to follow (Gita 5.02).

Jay: Doesn't the word renunciation usually mean leaving worldly possessions and living in an Ashram (monastery) or in a lonely place?

Grandma: The word Samnyāsa in the strict sense means renouncing (or giving up) all personal motives, worldly possessions and objects. But it also means living in society and serving society by doing one's duty without any personal motive. Such a person is called Karma-Samnyāsi.

Some spiritual leaders, such as Adi Shankarāchārya, consider the path of renouncing all worldly possessions as the highest path and the goal of life. He himself became a Samnyāsi when he was a young boy.

Lord Krishna says: "An enlightened person or a Samnyāsi (or hermit, one who has given up all personal motive) sees the Lord in all. Such a person looks at a learned person, an illiterate person, the rich, the poor, an outcast, even a cow, an elephant, or a dog with an equal eye." (Gita 5.18).

I am going to tell you the story of a great spiritual leader, hero, guru, Samnyāsi and thinker. His name is Adi Shankarāchārya. A student of the Gita owes him great respect and honor.

5. Adi Shankarāchārya

Adi Shankarāchārya (or Shankara) is the author and promoter of non-dualistic philosophy of Vedanta. It states that entire universe is nothing but an expansion of God. He was born in the state of Kerala in the year 788 A.D. By the age of eight, he had learned all four Vedas, and by the age of twelve, was well versed in all Hindu scriptures. He is believed to be Lord Shiva in human form.

Adi Guru Shankarāchārya

He wrote many books, including a commentary on the Bhagavad-Gita, Upanishads, BrahmaSutra and many others. The holy Bhagavad-Gita was hidden in Mahābhārata as a

Chapter before Shankara brought it out to us. Shankara took the Gita from Mahābhārata, gave it Chapter headings, and wrote the first commentary of the Gita in Sanskrit. The first English translation of the Gita was done by a British ruler of India in the 19th century.

Shankara established four main monasteries in different corners of India: at Shringeri, Badrināth, Dvārkā, and Puri. He stopped the spread of Buddhism over Hindu ideals, and restored Hinduism to its past glory. According to his non-dual philosophy, the individual soul (Jiva) is Brahma (God), and the world is the play of Māyā, the illusory kinetic energy of Brahma.

He certainly was a Self-realized man. But at first, he had the feeling of duality, of high and low caste. His faith in the absolute God (Brahma) was not very firmly established in his heart.

One day, he was going to the Shiva temple in the holy city of Banāras after bathing in the holy Gangā river. He saw an untouchable, a butcher, carrying a load of meat. The butcher came on his way and tried to touch Shankara's feet in respect.

Shankara shouted angrily: "Get out of the way! How dare you touch me? Now I have to take a bath again."

"Holy sir," said the butcher, "I have not touched you, nor have you touched me. The pure Self cannot be the body or the five elements out of which the body is created." (There are more details in Chapter 13.)

Then Shankara saw the vision of Lord Shiva in the butcher. Lord Shiva had Himself come to Shankara to firmly implant the non-dualistic philosophy in him. Shankara was a much better person from that day by the grace of Lord Shiva.

This story illustrates that equality with all beings is difficult to practice all the time. To have such a feeling is the mark of a truly God-realized person or a perfect Samnyāsi.

Chapter 5 summary: Lord Krishna considers the path of Selfless service (Sevā) to humanity without attachment to its results as the best path for most people. Both paths, the path of Self-knowledge and the path of Sevā, lead to a happy life here on the earth and Nirvāna after death. Samnyāsa does not mean leaving worldly possessions. It means not being attached to them. An enlightened person sees the Lord in all beings and treats everybody equally.

CHAPTER 6
PATH OF MEDITATION

Jay: Grandma, you said there are several paths leading to God. You told me about the path of duty and the path of spiritual knowledge. Please tell me about other paths.
Grandma: The third path is called the path of meditation.

One who is united with God is called a yogi. The mind of a yogi is peaceful and completely united with God. A yogi has control over his mind, senses, and desires. He is free from anger and greed. A clod, a stone, and gold are the same to a yogi, who sees God in everything and everything in God (Gita 6.08, 14.24). A yogi sees every being with an equal eye; whether a friend, enemy, hater, relative, saint, or sinner (Gita 6.09). The mind of a yogi remains calm even during the worst time (Gita 6.19).

Jay: Is there a method of meditation simple enough for children, Grandma?

Grandma: Yes, there is, Jay. The mind is your best friend as well as your worst enemy. The mind is a friend for those who have control over it and an enemy for those who do not control it (Gita 6.05-06). So you should try to control this friend. The mind is like wind, very restless and difficult to control, but you can control it by regular practice of meditation (Gita 6.34).

Guru Nanak said: Master the mind, and you master the world.

A Simple Method of Meditation

The best time to meditate is in the morning before going to school. Sit in your meditation or Poojā room. Hold your waist, spine, chest, neck, and head erect, motionless and steady. Close your eyes, take a few slow and deep breaths. Remember your favorite deity and ask his or her blessing. Mentally chant OM or AUM for few minutes. If your mind starts to wander here and there, bring it back gently to concentrating on your favorite deity.

There is a story of a child named Dhruva in our scriptures who got his wishes fulfilled using the path of meditation.

6. The Story of Dhruva

Dhruva was the son of king Uttānapāda and Suniti. King Uttānapāda was very fond of his second wife, Suruchi, and used to be mean to Suniti, Dhruva's mother. One day, when Dhruva was five years old, his step-brother was sitting on his father's lap. Dhruva also wanted to sit there. But his step-mother stopped him and dragged him aside.

She spoke rudely to Dhruva, saying: "If you want to sit on your father's lap, you should have been born to me instead of to your mother. At least now, pray to Lord Vishnu, so that He will make this happen."

Dhruva was deeply hurt by his step-mother's insulting words. He went to his mother, weeping. His mother consoled him and told him to take his step-mother's words seriously and pray to Lord Vishnu, who is the helper of all beings.

Dhruva left the kingdom for the forest with a determined mind to see Lord Vishnu and reach a higher place. On the way, he was met by the celestial sage Nārada. Nārada gave him the 12-syllable mantra: "Om namo bhagavate vāsudevāya" for worshiping the Vishnu form of Lord Krishna. Dhruva worshipped Vishnu for six months, and Lord Vishnu appeared before him. Vishnu promised that Dhruva's wishes would be fulfilled and he would reach the highest heavenly seat of the Polestar, which is not destroyed even when all the worlds are destroyed.

Dhruva returned to the kingdom. When the King grew old, he decided to crown Dhruva as the King. Dhruva ruled for many years and in the end reached the Polestar granted by Lord Vishnu. It is said that the entire Zodiac is made up of planets, stars, etc. All rotates around the Polestar. To this day, when Indians see the Polestar, they remember Dhruva, the devotee of perfect purity of mind and firm determination.

Jay: What happens to a yogi who does not become successful in this life?

Grandma: No spiritual practice performed by anybody ever goes to waste. The unsuccessful yogi is reborn into a rich or spiritually advanced family. The unsuccessful yogi regains the knowledge he had in the previous life and tries again to become perfect from where he or she left off. No spiritual effort is ever wasted.

Jay: How can I become the best yogi, Grandma?

Grandma: To be the best yogi, see all beings as yourself and feel their pain and pleasure as your own. Lovingly think of God with supreme faith, and always keep your mind set on Him (Gita 6.47).

Chapter 6 summary: The third path to God is yoga of meditation. To be the best yogi, see every being as yourself, and feel the pain and pleasure of others as your own. A very simple method of meditation uses the sound vibration of OM. No spiritual practice is ever wasted.

CHAPTER 7
KNOWLEDGE AND ENLIGHTENMENT

Jay: How was our whole universe formed, Grandma? Does it have a creator?

Grandma: There is a creator behind any creation, Jay. Nothing can be created without somebody or some power behind it. Some power is needed, not only to create it, but also to support and run it. We call that power God, the Absolute, the Supreme in English, and Krishna, Ishvara, Bhagavān, Shiva, Devi in Sanskrit. Other religions call that power by different names. In a real sense, God is not the creator of the universe, but He Himself becomes everything in the universe. He manifests as Brahmā, whom we call the creator. Actually, Brahmā and all other deities (gods and goddesses) are just names of different powers of the one and only One God. People think Hindus worship many gods and goddesses, but that is due to lack of their true knowledge.

The entire universe is a manifestation of God. This is the highest philosophy that you may not understand completely now.

All is manifestation of One God

Jay: How does one God become so many things in the universe?

Grandma: According to the Sāmkhya theory of creation, God's energy (Atmā or Spirit) itself becomes Nature or matter, made up of the five basic elements. The entire creation is born and sustained by different combinations of these two energies: Spirit and Matter (Gita 7.06). He is in the form of light in the Sun and the Moon; He is in the form of mind and strength in human beings. He digests our food and supports our life. We are all connected by the same Spirit as jewels in a necklace are connected by the same thread (Gita 7.07).

Jay: If God is everywhere and in everything, why doesn't everyone understand and love and worship Him?

Grandma: That is a good question, Jay. Generally, people have a false idea of God because everyone is not given the power to understand Him. Just as some people can't understand calculus or even elementary mathematics, so people who have no good Karma, can't know, understand, love, or worship God.

Jay: Then who are the ones who understand God?

Grandma: There are four types of people who worship or seek to understand God: (1) those who are sick or in some kind of trouble or seek help in doing well in their studies or work, (2) those who are trying to get the knowledge of God, (3) those who want money, and (4) the wise ones who know God (Gita 7.16). Lord Krishna considers all four types of people as devotees. The wise one is the best because a wise person worships God without wanting anything from Him. Even such wise ones completely know God only after many births (Gita 7.19).

Jay: If I worship Krishna, can I get good grades in an examination or get rid of sickness?

Grandma: Yes, He fulfills the desires of all who believe in Him and who always worship and pray with firm faith. God is both our Father and Mother. You should ask God what you want in a prayer. He fulfills the desires of His sincere devotees (Gita 7.21). But you also must work hard.

Jay: Then why doesn't everybody worship Krishna? Why do we worship Lord Ganesha, Shri Hanumāna, Mother Sarasvati and many other deities?

Grandma: Lord Krishna is the name of the Supreme God. Some sects of Hinduism call the Supreme God as Lord Shiva and Mother also. All other deities (gods) worshipped by us are a part of His power. Just as all rain water goes to the ocean, so worship of any deity goes to Krishna, the Absolute. But a beginner should chose just one of the many deities and establish a personal relationship by doing Poojā, or at least Namaskāra, everyday to the chosen deity. The personal deity then becomes your personal guide and protector. The personal deity is called IshtaDeva or IshtaDevi, your personal god.

Jay: You said that the entire universe is only another form of God. Is God formless or can God take forms?

Grandma: This big question not only confuses children, but also puzzles adults. Answers to this question created various sects or groups in Hinduism. One sect, called Arya

Samāj, believes that God cannot have forms and is formless. Another group believes God has a form. A third group believes God is formless and takes forms. Still others believe God is both with form and without form.

I believe everything has a form. Nothing in the world is formless. God has a form, which is invisible to our physical eyes. He cannot be understood by the human mind or described by words. Supreme Being has a transcendental (or out of this world) form and a Supreme Personality. He has no origin but is the origin of everything. He has no beginning, middle or end. The invisible God is the cause of the visible world. Invisible does not mean formless. Everything we see is another form of God.

Here is a story about practical application of seeing the Supreme in all beings as mentioned in Gita 7.19.

7. See God in All Beings

In a forest lived a holy man who had many disciples. He taught them to see God in all beings and to bow down before them. One day a disciple went into the forest to get wood for fire. Suddenly he heard a shout.

"Get out of the way! A mad elephant is coming!"

Everyone but the disciple of the holy man ran away. He saw the elephant as God in another form, so why should he run away from it? He stood still, bowed before the elephant, and began meditating on God in the form of the elephant.

The mahout (trainer) of the elephant shouted: "Run away! Run away!"

But the disciple didn't move. The animal grabbed him with its trunk, threw him to one side, and went on its way. The disciple lay unconscious on the ground. Hearing what had happened; his god-brothers came to him and carried him to the hermitage. With the help of some herbal medicine, he regained consciousness.

Then someone asked, "When you knew the mad elephant was coming, why didn't you leave the place?"

He answered: "Our guru has taught us that God is in all beings, animals as well as human. Therefore, I thought it was only the elephant-god that was coming, so I didn't run away."

At this the guru said: "Yes, my child, it is true that the elephant-god was coming; but the mahout-god asked you to get out of way. Why didn't you trust the mahout's words? Also, the elephant-god does not have the Self-knowledge that all are God!"

God dwells in all beings. God is even in the tiger; but you cannot hug the tiger on that account! Be close only with good people, and keep away from the evil-minded. Keep away from the unholy, the evil, and the impure.

8. The Unseen

One day a 6-year-old girl was sitting in a classroom. The teacher was going to explain evolution to the children.

The teacher asked a little boy: "Manav, do you see the tree outside?"

Manav: "Yes."

Teacher: "Manav, do you see the grass outside?"

Manav: "Yes."

Teacher: "Go outside and look up and see if you can see the sky."

Manav: "Okay. (He returned a few minutes later.) Yes, I saw the sky."

Teacher: "Did you see God anywhere?"

Manav: "No."

Teacher: "That's my point. We can't see God because he isn't there. He just doesn't exist."

A little girl spoke up and wanted to ask the boy some questions. The teacher agreed, and the little girl asked the boy:

"Manav, Do you see the tree outside?"
Manav: "Yes."
Little Girl: "Manav, do you see the grass outside?"
Manav: "Yessssss!"
Little Girl: "Did you see the sky?"
Manav: "Yessssss!"
Little Girl: "Manav, do you see the teacher?"
Manav: "Yes"
Little Girl: "Do you see her mind or her brain?"
Manav: "No"

Little Girl: "Then according to what we were taught today in school, she must not have a brain!"

God cannot be seen with our physical eyes. He can be felt by the eyes of knowledge, faith, and devotion only (Gita 7.24-25). For we walk by faith, not by sight. He answers our prayer!

Chapter 7 summary: There is only one God, who is called by many names. Devas, Devis, or deities in our religion are nothing but the names of different powers of One Absolute God. Deities are different names and forms of God's powers to help us worship and pray. Four types of people worship God. The entire creation is made up of five basic elements and the Spirit. God is both formless and with form. God can take any form. One cannot know the true nature of God unless one has spiritual knowledge.

CHAPTER 8
THE ETERNAL BRAHMA

Jay: I don't have a big spiritual vocabulary, Grandma, so I don't understand many words that I hear at the temple. Can you explain some of them in a simple way?

Grandma: I will explain some of the Sanskrit words, so listen very carefully. You may not completely understand these terms at your age.

The Spirit that is inside all living beings is called Brahma in Sanskrit. Brahma not only supports living beings but also supports the whole universe. This is the formless nature of God, the Absolute. Brahma is beginningless, endless (or everlasting) and changeless; therefore, it is also called Eternal Brahma. The word Brahma often gets confused with the word Brahmā, the creative force or creator of this universe. The word Brahma is also spelled as Brahma or Brahman. The word Brahman often gets mixed up with another term, Brāhmana, also spelled as Brāhmin, which refers to the upper caste or intellectual class of people in India. I will explain this term later in Chapter18.

ParaBrahma, Paramātmā, Father, Mother is the Supreme Being, who is the origin of everything, including Brahma (Spirit or Atmā) and the creator, Brahmā.

The word Karma has several meanings. Generally, it means to do or work. It also means the stored up fruits of one's work over past lives.

Various powers of Brahma are called Daiva (or Deva, Devi, Devatā). We worship these powers to get our worldly desires fulfilled.

Ishvara is the power of God that stays in the bodies of all living beings to guide and control us.

Bhagavān simply means powerful. This term is used for God. We call ShriKrishna also Bhagavān Krishna.

Jiva or Jivātmā means living beings that take birth, have a limited life span, and die or change form.

Jay: How often should I remember and worship God to make sure that I remember God when I die?

Grandma: We should form the habit of remembering God before taking our food, before going to bed, after getting up in the morning, and before starting any work or study.

Jay: Are we always reborn as human beings?

Grandma: Human beings can take any one of the 8.4 million life-forms on earth. Hindus believe in life after death. Lord Krishna said: "Whatever object one remembers at the time of death, that object one gets after death. During death, one remembers whatever thought existed during most of one's lifetime." (Gita 8.06). Therefore, one should always remember God and do one's duty (Gita 8.07).

Here is a story to illustrate the theory of transmigration of souls.

9. The Story of King Bharata

When Sage Vishvāmitra was busy creating his own universe; Indra, the King of heaven could not tolerate that. So he sent a beautiful heavenly dancer, Menakā, to disturb him from his work. She succeeded and bore sage Vishvāmitra's daughter, Shakuntalā. She was raised in the hermitage of sage Kanava after Menakā left for heaven.

One day a King named Dushyanta wandered in the hermitage of sage Kanava. There he met and fell in love with Shakuntalā, whom he secretly married in the hermitage. Afterwards, she gave birth to a baby boy named Bharata. He was very handsome and strong, even during his childhood. Bharata looked like the son of a Deva. When he was only six years old, he used to play in the jungle by tying up baby wild animals, such as tigers, lions, and elephants.

Bharata became the king after Dushyanta. Bharata was the greatest king of the land. Even today we also call India BhārataVarsha, the land of King Bharata. He had nine sons, but none of them seemed fit to rule after him, so he adopted a qualified child, who took over the kingdom after Bharata. Thus, King Bharata laid the foundation of democracy.

There have been several other rulers by the name of Bharata such as Bharata, the younger brother of Lord Rāma and Mahārāja Bharata. Here is a story of Mahārāja Bharata:

A devotee named Mahārāja Bharata, the son of a saintly King Rishabha Deva, also ruled over our entire planet. He ruled for many years but eventually renounced everything to take up spiritual life of an ascetic. Although he was able to give up his opulent kingdom, he became attached to a baby deer. Once when the deer was absent, Mahārāja Bharata was so disturbed that he began to search for it. While searching and lamenting the deer's absence, Mahārāja Bharata fell down and died. Because his mind was fully absorbed thinking of the deer at the time of his death, he naturally took his next birth from the womb of a deer.

This is the theory of transmigration of the soul, which we believe. Some western philosophers believe in reincarnation. The reincarnation theory is based on the assumption that a human soul takes birth only as humans, not as animals. The theory of transmigration seems more universal than the theory of reincarnation.

Jay: If living beings go through cycles of birth and death, how about the Sun, Moon, Earth, and stars? Do they also take birth and get destroyed?

Grandma: The entire cosmos (invisible or visible) has a life span of 311 trillion Solar years. During this period, the entire cosmos is destroyed and created again and again **(Gita 8.17-19, 9.07)**. But ParaBrahma is everlasting and is never destroyed. It remain in dormant state (Baby or subtle form) as shown below:

Only God remains after all is destroyed

Jay: If some people do not come back to this world after death, what happens to them? Do they go to heaven and live there forever?

Grandma: Those who have done good work here on earth go to heaven, but they have to come back after enjoying the pleasures of heaven (Gita 8.25, 9.21). Those who have been naughty and bad go to hell for punishment and also come back to earth. Those who have gained salvation (Nirvāna) do not take birth again. They become one with God and go to His Supreme Abode, called Parama-Dhāma). The Supreme abode is higher than heaven.

Jay: How can we gain the Supreme Abode, the house of God?

Grandma: Those who have the true knowledge of God are called God-realized and reach the house of God. They do not reincarnate. This is called the path of no return (Gita 8.24). This path is blocked for the ignorant and persons without the necessary qualities, such as austerity, faith in God, and knowledge of God. Only those who have these qualities will walk this path of no return. Those who have not realized God, but have done good work, go to heaven by virtue of their good Karma and take birth on earth again until they perfect themselves and become Self-realized (Gita 8.25).

Chapter 8 summary: Some of the common Sanskrit terms have been explained, which you will understand better as you grow older. The theory of transmigration and the cycle of creation and destruction of the universe were also explained. A very simple and easy method of God-realization is to always remember God and do your duty.

CHAPTER 9
KNOWLEDGE AND THE BIG MYSTERY

Jay: When God manifests on earth, does He act the same way as humans, or different from us?

Grandma: When God appears on earth, He does both human and divine acts called Lilā.

Now I will try to explain two doctrines of Hinduism

by example. Look at my gold chain, gold ring and this gold coin. They are all made of gold, so you can see them as gold. And you can see everything else made of gold as gold. They are different forms of gold. But you can also think of them as separate things — a chain, a ring, or a coin. The chain, the ring, and the coin are nothing but different shapes and forms of gold. In the same way, we can look at the Lord and His creation as nothing but an expansion of the Lord Himself. This viewpoint is known as non-dualistic (or Advaita) philosophy.

The other viewpoint sees God as one reality and creation as a different reality but dependent on God. This dualistic (or Dvaita) philosophy considers objects made of gold (such as a chain and a ring and a coin) different from gold (Gita 9.04-06).

Jay: Is that what people mean when they say God is everywhere and in everything?

Grandma: Yes, Jay, God is the Sun, the Moon, and the wind; fire, trees, earth, and stones, in the same way as everything made of gold is gold. That's why Hindus see and worship God in the stone and the tree as if these are God Himself in that form.

Jay: If everything comes from the Lord, then will everything become the Lord again, as everything made of gold can be melted into just gold again?

Grandma: Yes, Jay, the cycle of creation and destruction keeps on going. It's like turning my chain and ring and coin into gold again and then using the gold to make new jewelry and coins (Gita 9.07-08). The entire creation appears and disappears again and again.

Jay: If Lord is us, and we all come from the Lord, then why doesn't everyone love and worship Lord?

Grandma: Those who understand this truth worship God. They know the Lord is our Lord, and we are from Him, for Him, and we depend on Him, so they love and worship Him. But the ignorant do not understand or believe in universal God.

Jay: If I pray to God everyday and love Him and offer Him flowers or fruit, will He be pleased and help me in my studies?

Grandma: Lord Krishna said in the Gita that He takes care of all the needs of His devotees who worship Him with strong faith and loving devotion (Gita 9.22).

Jay: Does that mean that God loves only those who pray and worship Him?

Grandma: God loves all of us the same, but if we remember Him and pray to Him, we come closer to God. So we all should think of God, worship Him, meditate, and bow down to Him with faith, love, and devotion.

Jay: I would like to be close to the Lord Krishna, Grandma. How can I have more faith in Him and love Him more?

Grandma: Just think of all the nice things God does for us. He gives us so many different foods we enjoy. He gave us the Sun for heat and light. Look at the beautiful sky with the Moon, the stars and clouds in the night. This is all His beautiful creation, so think how beautiful the creator Himself must be! Worshiping God is saying thank you for His kindness. Praying is asking for what we need from God. Meditating is connecting with the Supreme power to get help and guidance.

Jay: If there is only one God who gives us everything, why do you have so many deities in your prayer (Poojā) room, Grandma? Why don't you just worship the one Lord Krishna?

Grandma: Lord Krishna said: "Those who worship other deities, also worship Me through those deities." (Gita 9.23). We can worship any deity we feel close to. That favorite deity is called IshtaDeva, our own personal god (or the guardian angel) who becomes our personal guide and protector.

Jay: Why do we offer fruits and flowers to God?

Grandma: Lord Krishna said in the Gita that anyone who offers Him a leaf, a flower, a fruit, water, or anything with love and devotion, He not only accepts it, but eats the offerings! (Gita 9.26). That's why we always offer our food to God with a prayer before we eat it. Food offered to God is called Prasāda or Prasādam. Anybody can reach God who worships Him with faith, love and devotion. This path of devotion is open to all of us.

Here is a story about the power of faith.

10. A Boy Who Fed God

A noble man used to worship his family's deity everyday with food offerings. One day he had to go out of his village for the day. He said to his son, Raman: Give the offering to the deity today. See that God is fed.

The boy offered food to the deity in the shrine, but the image would neither eat nor drink nor talk. Raman waited a long time, but still the image did not move. But he totally believed that God would come down from His throne in heaven, sit on the floor and eat.

Again and again he prayed to the deity, saying: "O Lord, please come down and eat the food. It is already very late. Father will get angry if I did not feed you." The deity did not say a word.

The boy wept and cried: "O Lord, my father asked me to feed you. Why won't you come down? Why won't you eat from my hands?"

The boy wept for some time with a longing soul. At last the deity came down smilingly from the altar in human form and sat before the meal and ate it.

After feeding the deity, the boy came out of the prayer room. His relatives said: "The worship is over. Now bring the Prasādam for us."

The boy said: "God has eaten everything, He did not leave anything for you today."

They entered the prayer room and were speechless with wonder to see that the deity had really eaten every bit of the offering.

The moral of the story is that God does eat if you offer food with full faith, love, and devotion. Most of us don't have the faith Raman had. We don't know how to feed Him! It is said that we must have faith in God like a child or we shall not enter the supreme abode, the house of God.

Jay: Grandma, what if a person is a sinful thief or robber. Can that person also love God?

Grandma: Yes, Jay. Lord Krishna has said in the Gita: If even the most sinful person decides to worship Me with loving devotion, such a person soon becomes a saint because he or she has made the right decision (Gita 9.31).

Here is a story about such a robber.

11. The Great Highway Robber-Sage

We have two very popular epics or historical tales. The first one is the Holy Rāmāyana. The other one is Mahābhārata. The Bhagavad-Gita is a part of the Mahābhārata. It was written about 3,100 years B.C.E. Originally, the Holy Rāmāyana may have been written about 1.75 million years ago, according to latest findings of NASA. The original writer of Rāmāyana was a sage named Vālmiki. After Vālmiki, many other saints such as Tulasidas have written Rāmāyana, the story of Lord Rāma that all children should read. The legend is that Vālmiki was given the power by sage Nārada to write the entire episode before the event actually happened.

In the early part of his life, Vālmiki was a great highway robber. He made a living by robbing travelers. One day, the great celestial saint Nārada was passing by when Vālmiki attacked him and tried to rob him. Nārada asked Vālmiki why he was doing that. Vālmiki said that this is how he supported his family.

The sage told Vālmiki: "When you rob a person, you commit sin. Do your family members want to share that sin also?"

The robber replied: "Why not? I am sure they do."

The sage said: "All right, go home and ask everyone if they will share your sins along with the money you are bringing home."

The robber agreed. He tied the sage against a tree and went home and asked each member of his family, saying: "I bring you money and plenty of food by robbing people. A sage told me that it is sinful to rob people. Will you share my sins?"

No one in his family was willing to share his sin. They all said: "It is your duty to support us. We can't share your sin."

Vālmiki realized his mistakes and asked the sage what to do to atone for his sins. The sage gave Vālmiki the most powerful and the simplest "Rāma" mantra to chant and taught him how to worship and meditate. The highway robber gave up his sinful activity and soon became a great sage and writer by the grace of guru Nārada, the power of mantra, and his sincere spiritual practice.

Here is another story, Jay, that you should always remember. It illustrates the verses of the Gita that say Lord Krishna takes care of all of us (Gita 9.17-18).

12. The Footprints

One night, a man had a dream. He dreamed he was walking along the beach with the Lord. Across the sky he saw scenes from his life. For each scene, he noticed two sets of footprints in the sand; one belonging to him, and the other to the Lord.

When the last scene of his life came before him, he looked back at the footprints in the sand. He noticed that many times along the path of his life there was only one set of footprints. He also noticed that it happened at the very lowest and saddest times in his life.

This really bothered him, and he questioned the Lord about it.

"Lord, You said that there is no one hateful or dear to You, but You are always with those who worship You with love and devotion (Gita 9.29). I have noticed that during the most troublesome times in my life, there is only one set of footprints. I don't understand why, when I needed You most, You left me alone."

God is always with you

The Lord replied, "My dear child, you are my own soul. I love you, and I would never leave you, even if you leave Me sometimes. During your time of trial and suffering, when you see only one set of footprints, that was because then I carried you. When you have trouble, it is caused by your own Karma. That is when you are tested and can grow stronger."

The Lord Krishna said in the Gita: "I personally take care of the needs of devotees who always remember and love Me." (Gita 9.22).

Chapter 9 summary: The dualistic philosophy sees God as one reality and creation as a different reality dependent on Him. Non-dual philosophy sees God and His creation as One. God loves all of us the same, but He takes personal interest in His devotees because such a person is closer to Him. It is like one gets more heat if one sits close to the fire. There is no unforgivable sin or sinner. The fire of sincere repentance burns all sins.

CHAPTER 10
MANIFESTATION OF GOD

Jay: If Lord Krishna said He will take care of us if we always remember and adore Him, then I want to know and love God. How do I do that, Grandma?

Grandma: The love of God is called devotion (Bhakti). If you have devotion, God will give you the knowledge and understanding of the Self (Gita 10.10). The more you know and think about God's glory, power and greatness, the stronger your love will grow. Thus the knowledge and love of God go together.

Jay: God is so great, and powerful, how can I really know Him?

Grandma: Nobody can fully know God. He is the cause of cosmic energy and power, a cause that will remain a big mystery. God is unborn, without beginning or end. Only God can really know God! (Gita 10.15). If anyone says, I know God, that person does not know. Anyone who knows the Truth says: I do not know God.

Jay: Then what can we know about God, Grandma?

Grandma: God knows everything, but nobody can know God. According to Shankara, the entire creation is nothing but another form of God. The creation has come out of God's energy called Māyā. Everything comes from Him and eventually goes back to Him. God is One, but has become many. He is everywhere and in everything (Gita 10.19-39). He is the Generator or creator (Brahmā), Operator or maintainer (Vishnu), and Destroyer (Mahesha) of all beings. He creates everything, including the sun, moon, stars, wind, water, air, fire, and even our thoughts, feelings, intellect, and other qualities. We can see His glory and greatness throughout creation. The beautiful sky with earth and all the planets you see is only a small part of His glory. Seeing God everywhere purifies our mind and makes us a better person.

Here is a story about why we know very little about God (Gita 10.15).

13. The Four Blind Men

Four blind men went to see an elephant.

One touched the leg of the elephant and said, "The elephant is like a pole."

The second touched the trunk and said, "The elephant is like a thick club."

The third touched the belly and said, "The elephant is

like a big jar."

The fourth touched the ear and said, "The elephant is like a big hand fan."

Thus they began to quarrel amongst themselves as to the shape of the elephant.

A passer-by, seeing them thus quarreling, said, "Why are you all quarreling?" They told him the problem and asked him to be the judge.

The man said: "None of you has seen the elephant. The elephant is not like a pole; its legs are like poles. It is not like a thick club; its trunk is like a thick club. It is not like a big jar; its belly is like a big jar. It is not like a fan; its ear is like a fan. The elephant is all these — legs, trunk, belly, ears and much more."

In the same way, those who argue about the nature of God have known only a small part of His Reality. That's why sages say God is "neither this, nor that."

Jay: What about people who do not believe in God?

Grandma: Such people are called atheists or disbelievers. They do not believe in the existence of a creator because they cannot comprehend how such a cosmic person or power can exist. So they question and doubt the existence of God. Their doubts may be erased someday when they find a real spiritual master or guru by the grace of God. Atheists are those whose journey towards God has not yet begun. Doubts arise even in the minds of believers; therefore, just have faith, believe in God, and do your duty.

Chapter 10 summary: Nobody can know God, the Supreme Being, because He or She is the origin of all beings, the cause of all causes. Everything, including our body, mind, thoughts, and feelings, comes from God. He is the creator, supporter, and destroyer of all. He is infinite and has no beginning or end. The entire universe is the expansion of a tiny fraction of His energy (Gita 10.41-42). All deities are just the names of His various powers. Worshiping God with faith, using any name, form, and method gives us what we want and helps us become good and peaceful.

CHAPTER 11
THE VISION OF GOD

Jay: You said we can know a little bit about God. Is it possible for people to see God?
Grandma: Yes, Jay. But not with our physical eyes. God does not have hands and legs like we have in our world. But when God is pleased by our selfless service (Sevā) and devotion, He may appear in a vision in dream. He can show Himself in any form, or in the form of one's personal god (IshtaDeva).

Jay: Is there any other way to see God?

Grandma: The best way to see God is to feel His presence in everything because everything is part of God. Yogis see the whole world as God's expansion. Everything is just another form of God. Knowing this, we can see God all around us. The entire universe is God, and we are His children and His tools (Gita 11.33). God uses us to do His work. He is within all of us.

Here is a story about God being always with us, but we cannot see Him with our physical eyes (Gita 11.08).

14. God Is always with You

A man wanted to smoke and went to a neighbor's house to get fire to light his charcoal. It was in the dead of night, and the householder was asleep. After he had knocked and knocked, the neighbor finally came down to open the door.

At the sight of the man he asked, "Hello! What's the matter?"

The man replied, "Can't you guess? You know I am fond of smoking. I have come here to get fire to light my charcoal."

The neighbor said, "Ha! Ha! You are a fine neighbor, indeed! You took the trouble to come and do all this knocking at the door in the dead of night! Why? You have a lighted lantern already with you!"

What we seek is very near and all around us. Everything is God in different forms. Everything in creation is within His gigantic form!

Another way to see God is to develop devotion and good qualities. Lord Krishna said if we have no attachment, selfish desires, hatred, enmity, or violence towards any being, we can reach and see God (Gita 11.55).

Jay: Has anybody seen Krishna as God?

Grandma: Yes, many saints and sages have seen Lord Krishna in various forms. Mother Yashodā saw Krishna's cosmic form. Arjuna also wanted to see Krishna as God. Because Arjuna was a great soul and a very dear friend of Krishna, Lord showed him His cosmic form. What Arjuna saw is described in great detail in Chapter 11 of the Gita.

The Cosmic form of Lord Krishna

Here is a brief description of the cosmic form of Krishna that Arjuna saw. He saw the whole world with all gods, sages, Lord Shiva, as well as Lord Brahmā, seated on the lotus in the body of Krishna. Lord had many arms, mouths, stomachs, faces, and eyes. His body had no beginning or end. Bright light was shining all around Him. Arjuna also saw all his cousins, along with many other kings and warriors, quickly entering into Lord's fearful mouths for destruction. This cosmic form of Krishna was very frightful to see, so

Arjuna wished to see Krishna in the four-armed Vishnu form with a crown, holding a conch, discus, club and lotus in His hands. Krishna then showed His four-armed Vishnu form to Arjuna.

Afterwards, Krishna showed His beautiful human form and comforted Arjuna, who was afraid. Then Arjuna became peaceful and normal again. Lord Krishna said that He can be seen in this four-armed form only through devotion (Gita 11.54).

Chapter 11 summary: We cannot see God with our human eyes. We can see Him only in a vision or trance (Samādhi). We can also see Him all around us. The entire creation is nothing but the body of the creator, and we are part of the cosmic form of God.

CHAPTER 12
PATH OF BHAKTI

Jay: Should we worship or meditate every day, Grandma, or just on Sundays?

Grandma: Children should do some form of worship, prayer, or meditation everyday. Good habits must be formed early.

Jay: You said that God is formless but also has forms. Should I worship God as Rāma, Krishna, Shiva, Durgā, or should I worship a formless God?
Grandma: Arjuna asked Lord Krishna the same question in the Gita (Gita 12.01). Krishna told Arjuna that worship of God with a form with faith is easier and better for most people, especially for the beginners. But a true devotee has

faith in everything: the formless God, and God with a form, such as Rāma, Krishna, Hanumāna, Shiva, and the Divine Mother Kāli, Durgā.

Jay: How should I worship, Grandma?

Go to the worship or meditation room before going to school and pray. Sit straight, close your eyes, take a few slow and deep breaths, remember your IshtaDeva and ask his or her blessing. Focusing your mind on your IshtaDeva with eyes closed is called meditation. You may also silently repeat a mantra such as 'OM' or 'Rām, Rām, Rām, Rām, Rām' a few times.

**Jay: When I start to meditate, I can't concentrate my mind, Grandma. My
mind starts to go everywhere. What should I do?**

Grandma: Don't worry, this even happens to adults. Try to concentrate or focus again and again. With practice, you will be able to focus your mind well, not only on God but also on your study materials. This will help you get good grades. You can also pray to God and worship by offering fruits, flowers, etc. to your IshtaDeva with love. Also, remember the Lord of learning, such as Lord Ganesha, Hanumāna, or Mother Sarasvati before starting your studies. Don't be selfish. Work hard. Accept the results of your work without getting upset by bad results. Try to learn from your failures. Never give up and improve yourself.

Jay: Is that all I have to do, Grandma? Did Krishna say anything else?

Grandma: You should also develop good habits such as obeying your parents, helping others in need, not hurting anybody, being friendly to all, saying sorry or asking forgiveness if you hurt anyone, keeping your mind calm, being grateful to those who have helped you, and saying thank you. God loves and helps those who act in this way. Such people are called devotees or Bhakta (Gita 12.13-19). If you don't have any one of these good habits, try to develop them (Gita 12.20).

Jay: Is it possible for a child to be a Bhakta?

Grandma: I already told you the story of Dhruva. Now I will tell you the story of another child Bhakta. His name was Prahlāda.

15. The Story of Bhakta Prahlāda

Hiranyakasipu was the king of demons. He performed a very difficult spiritual practice, and Lord Brahmā gave him a boon that he could not be slain by man or beast. The boon made him arrogant, and he terrorized all the three worlds, saying that there were no gods other than himself and everybody must worship him.

He had a son named Prahlāda, a religious child who always worshipped Lord Vishnu. This angered his father greatly; he wanted to drive the thought of Vishnu from his son's mind, so he turned him to a strict teacher to train him to worship only Hiranyakasipu as God and not Vishnu.

Prahlāda not only refused to listen to the teacher, but started teaching the other students to worship Vishnu. The teacher was very angry and reported this to the King.

The King burst into his son's room, and shouted, "I hear you have been worshipping Vishnu!"

Trembling, Prahlāda said softly, "Yes father, I have."

"Promise me that you will not do that again!" demanded the king.

"I cannot promise," Prahlāda immediately answered.

"Then I will have you killed," shouted the King.

"Not unless it is the wish of Lord Vishnu," replied the child.

The King tried his best to get Prahlāda to change his mind, but nothing worked.

He then ordered his guards to throw Prahlāda into the ocean, hoping that would frighten Prahlāda into promising not to worship Vishnu anymore. But Prahlāda remained loyal to Vishnu and kept praying to Him in his heart with love and devotion. Guards tied him to a huge rock and threw him into the ocean. By God's grace, the rock fell away and Prahlāda floated safely to the surface of the water. He was surprised to see Vishnu on the shore.

Vishnu smiled at him and said, "Ask me anything you want."

Prahlad saw Lord Vishnu in meditation

Prahlāda, replied, "I don't want kingdom, wealth, heaven, or a long life. I just want the strength to always love You and never turn my mind away from You."

Lord Vishnu granted Prahlāda's wishes.

When Prahlāda returned to his father's palace, the King was stunned to see him alive.

"Who brought you out of the sea?" he demanded.

"Lord Vishnu," said the child, simply.

"Do not say that name before me," shouted his father. "Where is your Lord Vishnu? Show him to me," he challenged.

"He is everywhere," replied the child.

"Even in this pillar?" asked the King.

"Yes, even in this Pillar!" replied Prahlāda confidently.

"Then let him appear before me in whatever form he wants," cried Hiranyakasipu and broke the pillar with his iron club.

Out from within the pillar jumped a being called Narasimha, who was half man and half lion. Hiranyakasipu, stood helplessly before him. Frightened, he called out for help, but none came.

Narasimha picked up Hiranyakasipu and placed him on his lap, where he mauled his body and tore it apart. Thus Hiranyakasipu met his end.

God blessed Prahlāda for the deep faith he placed in Him. After the death of Hiranyakasipu, demons were crushed, and the Devas took over the world once again from demons. To this day, the name of Prahlāda is counted among the great devotees.

Chapter 12 summary: The path of devotional love of God is very easy to practice. This path consists of daily deity worship, offering fruits and flowers, singing hymns (Bhajans) in praise of the glory of God, and developing certain good habits.

CHAPTER 13
CREATION AND THE CREATOR

Jay: Grandma, I can eat and sleep and think and talk and walk and run and work and study. How does my body know how to do all this?

Grandma: The whole world, including our body, is made of five basic elements or matter. These elements are: earth, water, fire, air, and ether or an invisible element. We have eleven senses: five sense organs (nose, tongue, eye, skin, and ear); five organs of action (mouth, hand, leg, anus, and urethra); and a mind. We smell through our nose, taste through our tongue, see through the eyes, feel touch through skin, and hear through our ears. We also have a sense of feeling by which we feel pain and pleasure. All these give our body what it needs to work (Gita 13.05-06). The Spirit or Atmā inside our bodies is also called Prāna. It supplies power to the body to do all work. When Prāna leaves the body, we are dead.

Jay: You said God is the creator of the universe. How do we know there is a creator or God?

Grandma: There has to be a creator behind any creation, Jay. Somebody or some power made the car we drive and the house we live in. Somebody or some power created the sun, the earth, the moon and the stars. We call that person or power God or the creator of this universe.

Jay: If everything has a creator, then who created God?

Grandma: This is a very good question, Jay, but there is no answer. God has always existed and will always exist. God is the origin of everything, but God has no origin. Good Lord is the source of everything, but He or She has no source!

Jay: Then, what is God like, Grandma? Can you describe Him?

Grandma: It is impossible to describe God directly. The Supreme Being can only be described by parables, and in no other way. His hands, feet, eyes, head, mouth, and ears are everywhere. He can see, feel, and enjoy without any physical sense organs. He does not have a body like us. His body and senses are out of this world. He walks without legs, hears without ears, does all works without hands, smells without a nose, sees without eyes, speaks without a mouth, and enjoys all tastes without a tongue. His actions are wonderful. His greatness is beyond description. God is present everywhere at all times. He is very near (living in every cell of our body) as well as far away in His Supreme Abode. He is the creator (Brahmā), the sustainer (Vishnu) and the destroyer (Mahesha), all in one (Gita 13.13-16).

The best way to illustrate why no one can describe God (Gita 13.12-18). is the story of the salt doll.

16. The Salt Doll

Once a salt doll went to measure the depth of the ocean so it could tell others how deep the ocean was. But every time it got into the water, it melted. Now, no one could report the ocean's depth. That's how impossible it is for anyone to describe God. Whenever we try, we melt into the big, mysterious ocean of His reality.

We can't describe Brahma. In a trance we can know Brahma, but in trance reasoning and intellect stop altogether. This means one does not retain the memory of experiences in trance (Samādhi). One who knows Brahma becomes Brahma-like (Gita 18.55). and does not talk, just as the salt doll melted into the ocean and could not report the ocean's depth. Those who talk about God have no real experience. Thus, Brahma can only be experienced and felt.

After trance one cannot recall the experience and describe.

Jay: Then how can we know and understand God?

Grandma: You can't know God by mind and intellect. He can be known only by faith and belief. He can also be known by Self-knowledge. One and the same God lives in the body of all beings as spirit and supports us. That is why we must not hurt anybody and must treat everybody equally (Gita 13.28). Hurting anybody is like hurting your own Atmā. The spirit in the body is the witness, the guide, the supporter, the enjoyer, and the controller of all events (Gita 13.22).

Jay: What is the difference between the creator and His creation?

Grandma: From a non-dualistic point of view, there is no difference between the two. The difference between the creator and creation is like the difference between the sun and the sun's rays. Those who have Self-knowledge truly understand the difference between the creator and the creation and become God-realized (Gita 13.34). The entire universe is His expansion, and everything is nothing but Him. God is both creator and the creation, the protector and the protected, the destroyer and the destroyed. He is within us, outside us, near, far, and everywhere.

If God's blessing comes to you, He will let you know who you really are and what your real nature is like.

Here is a story how Supreme Soul becomes individual soul (Jiva), forgets its real nature and tries to finds out its real nature (Gita 13.21).

17. The Vegetarian Tiger

Once a tigress attacked a herd of sheep. She was pregnant and very weak. As she sprang on her prey, she gave birth to a baby tiger and died within a couple of hours. The baby tiger grew up in the company of the lambs. The lambs ate grass, so the baby tiger followed their example. When they made sounds, the baby tiger also made sounds like a sheep. Gradually it grew to be a big tiger. One day another tiger attacked the same herd of sheep. The tiger was surprised to see a grass-eating tiger in the herd. Running after it, the wild tiger at last grabbed the cub, and the grass-eating cub began to make sounds like a sheep.

The wild tiger dragged it to the water and said: "Look at your face in the water. It is just like mine. Here is a little meat. Eat it."

Saying this, the wild tiger put some meat into the vegetarian tiger's mouth. But the vegetarian tiger would not take it and began to make the sound of a sheep again. Gradually, however, it got the taste for blood and began to like the meat.

Then the wild tiger said: "Now you see, there is no difference between you and me. Come along and follow me into the forest. "

We have been thinking that we are this body which is limited in time and space. We are not this body. We are the all-powerful Spirit in the body.

Chapter 13 summary: Our body is like a miniature universe. It is made up of five basic elements and powered by the Spirit. Universe has one and the only one creator or the creative power behind it. We call that power by various other names. God cannot be known, seen, described, or understood by a human mind. The creator Himself has become the creation like the cotton has become the thread, the cloth, and the dress.

CHAPTER 14
THREE GUNAS OF NATURE

Jay: Grandma, sometimes I feel lazy, and at other times I am very active? Why is that?

Grandma: We all pass through different states in order to do certain things. These states or modes (Gunas) are three types: the mode of goodness (Sattva), the mode of passion (Rajas), and the mode of ignorance (Tamas). We come under the influence of these three modes. Sometimes one mode becomes more powerful than the other two.

The mode of goodness makes you peaceful and happy. In this mode you will study scriptures, will not harm anybody, and will work honestly. When you are in the mode of passion, you become greedy for wealth and power. You will work hard to enjoy material pleasures and will do anything to satisfy your selfish desires. When you are in the mode of ignorance, you can't tell the difference between right and wrong action, and will do sinful and forbidden activities. You become lazy and careless, lack intelligence, and have no interest in spiritual knowledge (Gita 14.05-09).

Jay: Do these three modes of nature control us, Grandma, or do we have control over what we do?

Grandma: Actually, these three modes are the doers of all the actions (Gita 3.27). When we are under the influence of the mode of goodness, we do good and right actions; under the influence of the mode of passion, we do selfish actions; and under the influence of the mode of ignorance, we do bad things or become lazy (Gita 14.11-13). We must rise above the three Gunas to attain liberation (Nirvāna) (Gita 14.20).

Jay: What are we like when we have risen above the three Gunas?

Grandma: When we have risen above the three Gunas, we are not affected by pain and pleasure, success and failure, and we treat everybody like ourselves. Such a person depends on nobody but God.

Jay: It must be very hard to rise above these three modes. How can I rise above the three Gunas, Grandma?

Grandma: To rise above the three Gunas is not very easy, but it can be done with a little effort. If you are under the mode of ignorance, you must stop being lazy, stop putting off what you should be doing, and start helping others. This will bring you to the mode of goodness. If you are under the mode of passion, you must give up being selfish and greedy and help others. This will bring you to the mode of goodness. After reaching the mode of goodness, you can rise above the three Gunas by devotion to God. Lord Krishna said: One who serves Me with love and devotion rises above the three Gunas and becomes fit for God-realization (Gita 14.26).

Here is a story about the nature of three Gunas.

18. Three Robbers on the Path

Once a man was going through a forest when three

robbers jumped on him and robbed him.

One of the robbers then said, "What is the use of keeping this man alive?"

He was about to kill him with his sword when the second robber stopped him, saying: "What is the use of killing him? Tie him to a tree and leave him here."

The robbers tied him to a tree and went away.

After a while, the third robber returned and said to the man: "I am sorry; are you hurt? I will untie you."

After setting the man free, the thief said: "Come with me. I will take you to the public highway."

After a long time, they reached the road.

Then the man said: "Sir, you have been very good to me. Come with me to my house."

"Oh no!" replied the robber, "I can't go there. The police will know it."

The forest is this world. The three robbers are the three Gunas: goodness, passion and laziness. It is they who rob us of Self-knowledge. Laziness wants to destroy us. Passion ties us to the world. Goodness frees us from the grasp of passion and laziness. Under the protection of goodness, we are rescued from anger, passion, greed, and laziness. Goodness also loosens the bonds of the world. But goodness is also a robber. It cannot give us the pure knowledge of God. It can only show us the path leading to the house of God. We have to rise above the three Gunas and develop love of God.

Chapter 14 summary: Mother Nature puts us into these three modes or gears to get her work done through us. Actually, all work is done by these three Gunas of nature. We are not the doers, but we are responsible for our actions because we are given a mind and free will to decide and choose between right and wrong action. You can escape the influence of three Gunas by sincere effort, devotion to God and His grace.

CHAPTER 15
THE SUPREME PERSON

Jay: Grandma, I am confused by the difference between Supreme Spirit, Spirit, Divine Beings and individual souls. Will you please explain them again?

Grandma: Yes, Jay, these are terms you should understand well.

The Supreme Spirit is also called the Supreme Person, the Supreme Being, the Supersoul, the Absolute, Father, Mother, God, Ishvara, and by many other names. The Supreme Spirit is called ParaBrahma, Paramātmā, ParamaShiva, or Krishna in Sanskrit. The Supreme Spirit is the source or the root of everything. There is nothing higher than the Supreme Spirit.

Spirit (Brahma or Atmā) is a part of the Supreme Spirit that expands and supports the entire cosmos.

Divine Beings (Devas, Devis), such as Vishnu, Brahmā, Mahesha, and many others, are the expansions of Brahma (Spirit).

Individual Souls (soul or Jiva), such as all living beings, are the expansions of Divine Beings.

The Supreme Spirit and Spirit do not change and last forever. Divine Beings come out of Spirit and have a very long life span. Individual souls or the living beings have a very limited life span.

If you compare the creation with a tree, then the Supreme Lord Krishna (the Supreme Spirit) is the root of the tree. Atmā or Brahma (also spelled as Brahman, Brahm) is the trunk of the tree. The cosmos are the branches of the tree, and the holy books, such as the Vedas, Upanishads, and Gita, Dhammapāda, Torah, Bible, Koran, etc. are its leaves. Individual souls, such as living beings, are the fruits and flowers of the tree. Do you see how everything is connected and part of the Supreme Being?

Jay: How about planets, such as the Sun, and the Moon and the stars?

Grandma: The entire visible world, such as the Sun, Moon, Earth, other planets, and galaxies, was created by Lord Brahmā and is supported by Lord Vishnu and is destroyed by Lord Shiva or Mahesha. Remember that Brahmā, Vishnu, and Mahesha are a part of the energy of the Spirit or Brahma. The light energy of the Sun also comes from Brahma, and Brahma is a part of the Supreme Being, Lord Krishna. The sages tell us that everything is nothing but another form of Lord Krishna, the Supreme Being. Krishna is inside and outside everything. He has actually become everything. The One has become all. He also comes to earth in human form to establish law and order (Dharma) when needed (Gita 4.07-08).

Here is a story when the Supreme Lord Himself incarnated as Krishna about 5,100 years ago.

19. A Story of Baby Krishna

Baby Krishna had an elder half-brother named Balarāma.

Both played together in the village of Gokul. Krishna's birth mother's name was Devaki. His father's name was Vasudeva. Krishna is also called Vāsudeva. Krishna spent His childhood years under the care of Aunty Yashodā. Both Balarāma and Krishna were the favorites of the village milkmaids. Their mothers loved them proudly. Yasodā and Rohini (Balarāma's mother) dressed their young boys colorfully, Krishna in yellow with a crown of peacock feathers in His hair, and Balarāma in blue. The two boys went from place to place, making friends wherever they went. Most of the time they got into a lot of trouble!

One day, they were playing outside with a few of the other village boys, digging in the dirt, making mud pies, and getting very dirty. After a while, one of the older boys ran to mother Yashodā and said, "Krishna has been a bad boy, He has been eating clay!" Yashodā was annoyed with her young son. She had also been hearing other complaints from villagers that Krishna had been stealing butter from their houses.

She came out of her house and asked Krishna angrily, "Did you really eat clay, Krishna? How many times have I told you not to put things in your mouth!"

**Mother Yashoda saw entire Cosmos in
Baby Krishna's mouth.**

Krishna didn't want to be punished, so he played a trick on
mother Yashodā. He opened His mouth wide and said, "See,
Mother, I haven't been eating anything. These boys are just
lying to get me in trouble."

Yashodā looked inside Krishna's mouth. There, in the
little boy's mouth, she saw the whole universe — Earth and
stars, the wide empty space, the entire galaxy and the Milky
Way, the oceans and the mountains, the Sun and the Moon.
All were contained within His mouth. She realized then that

Krishna was Lord Vishnu incarnate, and she was about to fall before Him and worship.

But Krishna didn't want her to worship Him. He just wanted her to love Him the way mothers love their children. He could have come to earth in any form to fight the demons, but He liked being a little boy to a mother and a father who had performed many difficult spiritual practices to have God as their child. Baby Krishna realized that His trick had been a big mistake!

Quickly, He spread His power of Māyā over her. The next minute Yashodā was holding her son as usual, with no memory at all of what she had just seen in Krishna's mouth.

You should read interesting stories of Krishna's adventures and tricks with village milkmaids when you get time. Here are some pictures:

Krishna, the butter thief

20. The Story of Shri RamaKrishna

The Lord came to this earth as RamaKrishna, born on February 18, 1836, in the village Kamarpukur of West Bengal. Most of the stories I have told you are from his "Tales and Parables of Shri RamaKrishna." Swami Vivekananda was one of his most famous disciples. Swami Vivekananda was the first Hindu monk who came to the

USA in 1893. He established the Vedanta Society in New York. RamaKrishna led a very simple life, depending on God for his daily food and other necessities of life. He would not accept any money. He was married to Sarada Ma, whom he treated like his mother and never had any child. Sarada Ma used to tell her disciples: "If you want peace of mind, do not look into others' faults; rather, look into your own. No one is a stranger; the whole world is your own." Sarada Ma also warned her disciples not to be too close with persons of the opposite gender, even if God came in that form. RamaKrishna worshipped Goddess Kali as his personal deity in a temple at Dakshineshvar near Kolkata. This temple still exists today.

Chapter 15 summary: The creation is changeable and does not last forever. It has a limited life span. Brahma or Atmā does not change and is eternal. It is the cause of all causes. Krishna is called ParaBrahma or the Supreme Being. He is also called the Absolute because He has no origin. He is the source of Brahma. Everything in the universe comes out of Brahma. The entire visible world and its creatures are created by Brahmā, the creative power of Brahma; sustained by Vishnu's sustaining power and destroyed by Mahesha.

CHAPTER 16
DIVINE AND DEMONIC QUALITIES

Jay: I meet different types of students in the class. How many types of people are there, Grandma?

Grandma: Generally, there are only two types (or castes) of people in this world, the good and the bad (Gita 16.06).

Most people have both good and bad qualities. If you have more good qualities, you are called a good person, and if you have more bad qualities, you are called a bad person.

Jay: If I want to be a good person, what qualities must I have?

Grandma: You must be honest, nonviolent, truthful, without anger, calm, without harmful talk, kind, not greedy, gentle, forgiving, and humble. These are also called divine qualities because they lead us to God.

Jay: What bad habits should I avoid?

Grandma: Hypocrisy, telling lies, arrogance, pride, jealousy, selfishness, anger, greed, harshness, ungratefulness, and violence — these are bad qualities because they lead us away from God. Bad qualities also lead us to do bad things and get us into trouble. Do not be friends with people who have bad qualities because they do not know what to do and what not to do. Always be grateful to those who have helped you. Ingratitude is a great sin for which there is no remedy.

Desire, anger, and greed are very destructive. Lord Krishna calls these the three gates to hell (Gita 16.21).

Here is a story about how greed leads to sorrow.

21. The Dog and the Bone

One day a dog found a bone. He picked it up in his mouth and went to a lonely corner to chew it. He sat there and chewed the bone for some time. Then the dog felt thirsty and picked up the bone in his mouth and walked over a small wooden bridge to drink water from the creek

When he saw his own reflection in the water, he thought there was another dog with a bone in the river. Becoming greedy, he wanted to have the other bone also. He opened his mouth to bark and take the bone from the other dog. As soon as he opened his mouth to grab the other bone, the bone dropped out of his mouth and fell into the creek. The dog realized his mistake, but it was too late.

Greed can be overcome by being satisfied with what one has. A satisfied person is a very happy person. A greedy person cannot find true peace and happiness in life.

Jay: How can I know what to do and what not to do?

Grandma: Follow your holy books, Jay. Saints and sages tell us what to do and what not to do in our holy books. Have faith in God, and listen to your parents and elders.

We should develop as many good habits as possible. But no one has only good habits and no bad habits. Good Lord usually puts good and bad habits in the same package.

Here is a story about how Queen Draupadi discovered this truth from her own experience.

22. The Story of Queen Draupadi

Draupadi was the common wife of five Pāndavas. She was the daughter of a Rishi in her past life. She was very beautiful and virtuous, but in her past life, due to her past Karma, she had been unable to get married. This made her unhappy. So she started austerity to please Lord Shiva. After a long and difficult austerity, she pleased Lord Shiva, who asked her to choose a blessing of her choice. She asked for a husband who would be very religious, strong, a very good soldier, good looking, and gentle. Lord Shiva granted her wish.

In the next life, she was married to five brothers, but she was not very happy with this strange situation. Draupadi was a great devotee of Lord Krishna, who knows the past, present and future of all beings. He knew of her sorrow and explained what she had asked for in her past life. Lord Krishna said it was impossible for one man to have all the qualities she wanted in her husband, so she was married to five husbands in this life, who shared all these qualities among them.

After hearing this explanation from the Lord Krishna Himself, she, her parents, and her five husbands cheerfully accepted what fate had given them and lived happily.

The moral of the story is that one cannot find a husband or wife with all good or bad qualities, so one must learn to live with whatever is given by fate. There is no perfect spouse because no one has only good habits and no bad habits.

Chapter 16 summary: Generally, there are only two types of human beings: the good or divine and the bad or demonic. Most people have both good and bad qualities. Getting rid of bad habits and cultivating good habits are necessary for spiritual progress.

CHAPTER 17
THREE TYPES OF FAITH

Jay: Grandma, how do I know what foods to eat?

Grandma: There are three types of foods, Jay (Gita 17.07-10). The foods that bring long life, virtue, strength, health, happiness, and joy are juicy, smooth, substantial, and nutritious. Such health foods are the best. They are called Sattvik or healthy food.

Foods that are very bitter, sour, salty, hot, oily, and

acidic are called Rājasika or undesirable foods. Such junk foods are unhealthy, cause diseases, and should be avoided.

Foods that are not well cooked, spoiled, tasteless, rotten, burned, left-over, and impure (such as meat and alcohol) are called Tamasik or bad foods. One should not eat such foods.

Jay: How should I speak to others?

Grandma: You should never tell a lie. Your words should not be harsh, bitter, nasty, or insulting. They should be sweet, useful, and truthful (Gita 17.15). One who speaks politely wins the heart of all and is liked by everybody. A wise person should speak the truth if it is helpful and keep quiet if it is harsh. To help those in need is the universal teaching.

Jay: How should I help others?

Grandma: It is our duty to help those who are less fortunate and can't help themselves. Help anyone who needs help, but never expect anything in return. Charity is not only the best, but also the only use of wealth. We all should help a good cause. Give back what belongs to the world. But there are responsibilities. Money given in charity should be earned by lawful means. And we must make sure that the receiver is not a person likely to use the gift for evil purposes (Gita 17.20-22).

Jay: Will God give us what we want if we sincerely pray for it?

Grandma: Full faith in God makes things happen. There

is nothing impossible for faith. Faith works miracles. One must have faith before starting any work. It is said in the Gita that we can become whatever we want to be if we always think about it and pray to God with faith (Gita 17.03). Always contemplate about what you want to be, and your dream can come true.

Here is a story about a crow that had faith.

23. The Thirsty Crow

It was a hot summer day. A crow was very thirsty. He flew from place to place looking for water. He could not find water anywhere. Ponds, rivers, and lakes were all dry. The water in the well was too deep. Crow was very thirsty for water. He flew and flew. He was getting both tired and thirsty, but he did not give up the search.

At last he thought death was near and remembered God and started to pray for water. He saw a pitcher of water near a house. This made him very happy as he thought there must be water in the pitcher. He sat on the top of the pitcher and looked into it. To his great frustration he found that the water was at the bottom of the pitcher. He could see the water, but his beak could not reach the water. He became very sad and started to think how he could reach the water. Suddenly an idea came into his mind. There were stones near the pitcher. He picked up stones from the ground, one by one, and started dropping them into the pitcher. The water began coming up. Soon the crow could reach it easily. He drank the water, thanked God, and happily flew away.

Thus it is said, "Where there is a will, there is a way." The crow did what we all should do. He did not give up. He had faith that his prayer would be answered.

Here is another good story:

24. The Rabbit and the Turtle

A turtle always moves very slowly. His friend, the rabbit, often laughed at the slow turtle. One day, the turtle could not bear the insults and challenged the rabbit to run a race with him. All the animals in the jungle laughed at the idea because a race is usually between equals. A deer volunteered to be the judge.

The race started. The rabbit ran fast, and soon he was ahead of the turtle. As the rabbit came closer and closer to the winning post, he felt sure of winning. He looked back at the slow moving turtle, who was far behind.

The rabbit was so sure of winning that he thought, "I will sit under the tree and wait for the turtle. When he comes here, I shall run fast and cross the finish line before he does. This will make turtle angry, and it will be fun to see the turtle insulted."

The rabbit then sat under a tree. The turtle was still far behind. A cool wind was blowing gently. After some time passed, the rabbit fell asleep. When he woke up, he saw the turtle crossing the finish line. The rabbit had lost the race! All the animals in the jungle were laughing at the rabbit, and he learned a valuable lesson:

"Slow and steady wins the race."

You can succeed in any work if you work hard with strong faith. Be enthusiastic about what you want, and you will get it. We are the creator of our own fate. Thoughts create our future. We become what we always think of. So never think a negative thought or allow doubt to enter your mind. Keep working toward your goal. You cannot get anything through laziness, negligence, and delay. Keep your dream alive in your heart, and it will come true. All difficulties can be removed by faith in God and a firm determination to succeed. But the fruits of success must be shared with others. If you want your dream to be fulfilled, help fulfill someone else's dream!

Here is a story of a man who learned that God helps those who help themselves.

25. A Man Who Never Gave Up

Yava was the son of a sage who practiced hard penance to get the blessings of Indra, the King of Devas. He tortured his body with austerities and thus awakened the sympathy of Indra. Indra came before him and asked why he was hurting his body.

Yava answered: "I wish to be a great scholar of the Vedas. It takes a long time to learn the Vedas from a teacher. I am practicing austerities to get that knowledge directly. Bless me."

Indra smiled and said: "Son, you are on the wrong path. Return home, find a good teacher, and learn the Vedas from him. Austerity is not the way to learn; the path is study and study alone." With these words, Indra went away.

But Yava would not give up. He did his course of spiritual practice (austerities, penance) with even greater effort. Indra again came before Yava and warned him again. Yava announced that if his prayer was not answered, he would cut off his arms and legs one by one and offer them to the fire. No, he would never give up. He continued his penance. One morning, during his austerities, when he went to bathe in the holy Gangā River, he saw an old man on the bank throwing handfuls of sand into the river.

"Old man, what are you doing?" asked Yava.

The old man replied: "I am going to build a dam across the river so people can cross the river easily. See how difficult it is now to cross it. Useful work, isn't it? "

Yava laughed and said: "What a fool you must be to think you can build a dam across this mighty river with your handfuls of sand! Go home and do some other useful work."

The old man said: "Is my work more foolish than yours of learning the Vedas, not by study, but by austerities?"

Yava now knew that the old man was Indra. Yava earnestly begged Indra to grant him learning as a personal wish.

Indra blessed him and comforted Yava with the following words: "I grant you the wish you want. Go and read the Vedas; you will become learned."

Yava studied the Vedas and became a great scholar of the Vedas.

The secret of success is to keep thinking about what you want all the time and never give up until you get what you want. Do not let negative thoughts, such as delaying to start work, laziness, and carelessness stand in your way.

Before starting or ending any work or study, repeat OM TAT SAT, the threefold names of Brahma.

Jay: What does OM TAT SAT mean, Grandma?

Grandma: It means Krishna, the Almighty God, only exists. OM is used before starting any work or study. OM TAT SAT or OM Shantih, Shantih, Shantih, is also used at the end of any act.

Chapter 17 summary: There are three types of food — Sāttavik, Rājasik and Tāmasik — and they affect our well-being. Tell the truth in a pleasant way. Give charity to a deserving candidate, and give it wisely to avoid its misuse. You can become whatever you want to be if you work hard towards your goal.

CHAPTER 18
NIRVAVA BY GIVING UP EGO

Jay: Grandma, I am confused by different terms you used. Please explain to me clearly what is the difference between renunciation (Samnyāsa) and selfless work (KarmaYoga)?

Grandma: Some people think renunciation means walking away from family, home, possessions, and living in a cave or the forest or any other place outside society. But Lord Krishna defined Samnyāsa as giving up selfish motives behind all work (Gita 6.01, 18.02). In KarmaYoga one gives up (selfish) desire of enjoying the results of one's work. Thus a Samnyāsi is an advanced KarmaYogi who does not do anything for personal benefit. **True Samnyāsa is giving up of the ego and it leads to Nirvana or Moksha.**

Jay: What is ego, Grandma?

Grandma: Ego generally means pride or very high opinion about oneself. In a spiritual sense in the Gita it means the notion that a person is the doer, owner and enjoyer; when in a true sense Lord is the doer, owner of everything in the cosmos as well as the enjoyer. We all are just His instruments or tools; and trustees of all we own (Gita 11.33). Nirvana is not possible without giving up of the ego. And giving up of the ego is not possible without true spiritual knowledge of the Gita. Lord made ego to run the affairs of the society, but we must give up ego before we leave this world.

Jay: Does that mean I can't do anything for myself that gives me pleasure?

Grandma: That depends on what kind of pleasure you have in mind. Actions such as smoking, drinking, gambling, and taking drugs appear enjoyable in the beginning, but definitely produce harmful results in the end. Poison may taste delicious when you drink it, but you know its deadly results when it is too late. On the other hand, actions, such as meditation, worship, and helping the needy, seem difficult or boring in the beginning, but give very useful results in the end (Gita 5.22, 18.38). A very good rule to follow is to avoid any activity that seems pleasurable in the beginning but causes harmful effects in the end.

Jay: What kinds of activities in society are available, Grandma?

Grandma: In the ancient Vedic way of living, activities of human beings were divided into four universal types of human labor described by Lord Krishna (Gita 4.13, 18.41-

44). These four divisions — Brāhmana, Kshatriya, Vaishya, and Shudra — were based on the mental, intellectual, and physical abilities of persons. The worth of the individual — not the birth or social level one was born into — was the deciding factor. But these four orders are often mistaken for the caste system of modern times in India and elsewhere. The caste system is based on birth only.

Those who were interested in learning, teaching, preaching, and guiding people in spiritual matters were called Brāhmanas or intellectuals. Those who could defend the country, establish law and order, prevent crime, and administer justice were called Kshatriyas, the warriors. Those who were good in farming, cattle-raising, business, trade, finance, commerce, and industry were known as Vaishyas or businessmen. Those who were very good in service and labor work were classed as Shudras or workers.

People are born with certain abilities or could develop them through training and effort. Birth into a family at a certain social level, whether high or low, does not decide one's worth.

The four Varna system was work assigned according to individual's skills and ability. Unfortunately, the four work classifications became degraded into hundreds of rigid castes to the detriment of this great Dharma. Swami Vivekananda considers modern day caste system in India as a big blot on the face of our great way of life (Dharma). Even some of our educated immigrants from India (NRIs) are forming caste-based associations here in the USA !

Jay: How can anybody living and working in society attain liberation?

Grandma: Work becomes worship when done as a service

to the Lord and without selfish attachment to the results. If you work honestly for which you are suited, you incur no Kārmic reaction and attain God.

If you take on work that was not meant for you, such work produces stress, and you will not be very successful. It is important to find proper work that best suits your own nature. So you should know yourself before you can decide on the job that will be suitable for you (Gita 18.47). Then your work will not produce stress and will encourage creativity.

There is no perfect job. Every job has some faults (Gita 18.48). You should not be concerned about such faults in your duty in life. You can attain God by doing your duty with devotion to God and keeping your senses under control by some spiritual practice.

The following story illustrates that one can attain Self-realization by sincerely doing one's duty (Gita 18.46-58).

26. I am no Crane

A holy man named Kaushika had acquired great spiritual powers. One day, he sat under a tree meditating. A crane at the top of the tree soiled his head with its droppings. Kaushika looked up at it angrily, and his angry look killed the bird instantly. The holy man was pained when he saw the dead bird lying on the ground.

Some time later, he went as usual to beg for food and stood before the door of a house. The housewife was busy serving her husband with food and seemed to forget the holy man waiting outside. After her husband had been fed, she came out with food, saying, "I am sorry to have kept you waiting long. Forgive me."

But Kaushika, burning with anger, said: "Lady, you

have made me wait for a long time. This is not fair."

"Kindly forgive me," said the woman. "I was serving my sick husband and hence the delay."

"It is good to attend the husband," replied Kaushika, "but you seem to be an arrogant woman."

"I kept you waiting only because I was dutifully serving my sick husband," she replied. "Please do not be angry with me. I am no crane to be killed by your angry thought. Your anger cannot harm a woman who devotes herself to service of her husband and family."

Kaushika was surprised. He wondered how she knew of the crane incident.

She continued: "O great one, you do not know the secret of duty, or that anger is the greatest enemy that dwells in human beings. Go to the village Rampur in Mithilā and learn the secrets of doing one's duty with devotion from Vyādha Rāj"

Kaushika went to the village and met the man named Vyādha Rāj. He was surprised to learn he was selling meat at a butcher's shop. The butcher got up from his seat and asked: "Honored sir, are you well? Did that pure lady send you to me? I know why you have come. Let us go home."

The butcher took Kaushika to his house where Kaushika saw a happy family and was greatly amazed at the love and respect with which the butcher served his parents. Kaushika took his lesson from the butcher on doing one's duty. Vyādha Rāj did not kill the animals; he never ate meat. He just carried on his family business after his father retired.

Afterwards, Kaushika returned to his house and began to serve his parents, a duty which he had neglected before.

The moral of this story is that you can reach spiritual perfection by honestly doing whatever duty is yours in life.

This is a true worship of God (Gita 18.46).

Lord Krishna lives within all of us and guides us to work out our own Karma (Gita 18.61). Put forth your best effort, and gladly accept the results as His will. This is called surrendering to God or giving up of the ego (Gita 18.66). The gift of spiritual knowledge is the best gift because the absence of spiritual knowledge is the cause of all evil in the world. Spreading spiritual knowledge is the highest devotional service to Lord Krishna (Gita 18.68-69).

Everlasting peace and wealth are possible only when you do your duty well and also have the spiritual knowledge given in the Holy Gita by Lord Krishna (Gita 18.78).

Chapter 18 summary: Lord Krishna said that there is no real difference between a KarmaYogi and Samnyāsi. A KarmaYogi gives up the selfish attachment to the fruits of work, whereas a Samnyāsi does not work for any personal gain at all. There are two types of pleasures — helpful and harmful. Society has different work to suit different people.

One should choose work wisely. You can get God-realization while living in society by following the three D's— Duty, Discipline and Devotion to God.

This book is offered to Lord Shri Krishna. May He bless all those--who study it regularly and practice the teachings--with Goodness, Prosperity, and Peace.

OM TAT SAT